SCALE
DEVELOPMENT

Applied Social Research Methods Series
Volume 26

APPLIED SOCIAL RESEARCH METHODS SERIES

Series Editors:
LEONARD BICKMAN, Peabody College, Vanderbilt University, Nashville
DEBRA J. ROG, Vanderbilt University, Washington, DC

SCALE DEVELOPMENT

Theory and Applications

Robert F. DeVellis

Applied Social Research Methods Series
Volume 26

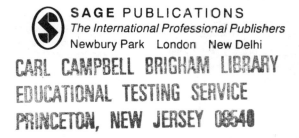

SAGE PUBLICATIONS
The International Professional Publishers
Newbury Park   London   New Delhi

To Brenda

For information address:

SAGE Publications, Inc.
2455 Teller Road
Newbury Park, California 91320

SAGE Publications Ltd.
6 Bonhill Street
London EC2A 4PU
United Kingdom

SAGE Publications India Pvt. Ltd.
M-32 Market
Greater Kailash I
New Delhi 110 048 India

Printed in the United States of America

Library of Congress Cataloging-in-Publication Data

DeVellis, Robert F.
  Scale development: theory and applications / Robert F. DeVellis.
      p.   cm. — (Applied social research methods series; v. 26)
  Includes bibliographical references and index.
  ISBN 0-8039-3775-X. — ISBN 0-8039-3776-8 (pbk.)
  1. Scaling (Social sciences) I. Title. II. Series.
H61.27.D48   1991
300′.72—dc20   91-10257
                                                                  CIP

FIRST PRINTING, 1991

Sage Production Editor: Michelle R. Starika

Contents

1

Overview

Measurement is of vital concern across a broad range of social research contexts. For example, consider the following hypothetical situations:

1. A health psychologist faces a common dilemma: the measurement scale she needs apparently does not exist. Her study requires that she have a measure that can differentiate between what individuals *want* to happen and what they *expect* to happen when they see a physician. Her research shows that previous studies used scales that inadvertently confounded these two ideas. No existing scales appear to make this distinction in precisely the way that she would like. Although she could fabricate a few questions that seem to tap the distinction between what one wants and expects, she worries that "made up" items might not be reliable or valid indicators of these concepts.

2. An epidemiologist is unsure how to proceed. He is performing secondary analyses on a large data set based on a national health survey. He would like to examine the relationship between certain aspects of perceived psychological stress and health status. Although no set of items intended as a stress measure was included in the original survey, several items originally intended to measure other variables appear to tap content related to stress. It might be possible to pool these items into a reliable and valid measure of psychological stress. However, if the pooled items constituted a poor measure of stress, the investigator might reach erroneous conclusions.

3. A marketing team is frustrated in its attempts to plan a campaign for a new line of high-priced infant toys. Focus groups have suggested that parents' purchasing decisions are strongly influenced by the apparent educational relevance of toys of this sort. The team suspects that parents who have high educational and career aspirations for their infants will be more attracted to this new line of toys. Therefore, the team would like to assess these aspirations among a large and geographically dispersed sample of parents. Additional focus groups are judged to be too cumbersome for reaching a sufficiently large sample of consumers.

In each of these situations, people interested in some substantive area have come head to head with a measurement problem. None of these researchers is interested primarily in measurement per se. However, each must find a way to quantify a particular phenomenon before tackling the main research objective. In each case, "off-the-shelf" measurement tools are either inappropriate or unavailable. All the researchers recognize that adopting haphazard measurement approaches runs the risk of yielding inaccurate data. Developing their own measurement instruments seems to be the only remaining option.

Many social science researchers have encountered similar problems. One all-too-common response to these types of problems is reliance on existing instruments of questionable suitability. Another is to assume that newly-developed questionnaire items that "look right" will do an adequate measurement job. Uneasiness or unfamiliarity with methods for developing reliable and valid instruments and the inaccessibility of practical information on this topic are common excuses for weak measurement strategies. Attempts at acquiring scale development skills may lead a researcher either to arcane sources intended primarily for measurement specialists or to information too general to be useful. This volume is intended as an alternative to those choices.

GENERAL PERSPECTIVES
ON MEASUREMENT

Measurement is a fundamental activity of science. We acquire knowledge about people, objects, events, and processes by observing them. Making sense of these observations frequently requires that we quantify them—i.e., that we measure the things in which we have a scientific interest. The process of measurement and the broader scientific questions it serves interact with one another; the boundaries between them are often imperceptible. This happens, for example, when a new entity is detected in the course of trying to measure something else entirely or when the reasoning involved in determining how to quantify a phenomenon of interest sheds new light on the phenomenon itself. For example, Gerrity, DeVellis, and Earp (1990) set out to assess physicians' reactions to uncertainty in medical practice. The scale development process revealed two distinct and unanticipated facets of physicians' reactions: stress from uncertainty and reluctance to disclose uncertainty. In essence, measurement can become a science in its own right, a subspecialty of the larger domain of inquiry.

Duncan (1984) argues that the roots of measurement lie in social processes and that these processes and their measurement actually precede science: "All measurement . . . is social measurement. Physical measures are made for social purposes" (p. 35). In reference to the earliest formal social measurement processes, such as voting. census-taking, and systems of job advancement, Duncan notes that "their origins seem to represent attempts to meet everyday human needs, not merely experiments undertaken to satisfy scientific curiosity." He goes on to say that similar processes "can be drawn in the history of physics: the measurement of length or distance, area, volume, weight and time was achieved by ancient peoples in the course of solving practical, social problems; and physical science was built on the foundations of those achievements" (p. 106).

Whatever the initial motives, each area of science develops its own set of measurement procedures. Physics, for example, has developed specialized methods and equipment for detecting subatomic particles. Within the behavioral/social sciences, *psychometrics* has evolved as the subspecialty concerned with measuring psychological and social phenomena. Typically, the measurement procedure used is the questionnaire, and the variables of interest are part of a broader theoretical framework.

HISTORICAL ORIGINS OF
MEASUREMENT IN SOCIAL SCIENCE

Ancient examples. Common sense and historical record support Duncan's claim that social necessity led to the development of measurement before science emerged. No doubt, some form of measurement has been a part of our species' repertoire since prehistoric times. The earliest humans must have evaluated objects, possessions, and opponents on the basis of characteristics such as size. Duncan (1984) cites biblical references to concerns with measurement (for example, "A false balance is an abomination to the Lord, but a just weight is a delight," Proverbs 11:1) and notes that the writings of Aristotle refer to officials charged with checking weights and measures. Anastasi (1968) notes that the Socratic method employed in ancient Greece involved probing for understanding in a manner that might be regarded as knowledge testing. In his 1964 essay, P. H. DuBois (reprinted in Barnette, 1976) describes the use of civil service testing as early as 2200 B.C. in China.

Emergence of statistical methods and the role of mental testing. Nunnally (1978) points out that, although systematic observations may have been going on, the absence of statistical methods hindered the development of a science of measuring human abilities until the latter half of the nineteenth century. Similarly, Duncan (1984) observes that, in most fields of mathematics other than geometry, applications preceded a formal development of the foundations (which he ascribes to the nineteenth century) by millennia. The eventual development of suitable statistical methods in the nineteenth century was set in motion by Darwin's work on evolution and his observation and measurement of systematic variation across species. Darwin's cousin, Sir Francis Galton, extended the systematic observation of differences to humans. A chief concern of Galton was the inheritance of anatomical and intellectual traits. Karl Pearson, regarded by many as the "founder of statistics" (e.g., Allen & Yen, 1979, p. 3), was a junior colleague of Galton's. Pearson developed the mathematical tools, including the Product-Moment Correlation Coefficient bearing his name, needed to examine systematically relationships among variables. Scientists could then quantify the extent to which measurable characteristics were interrelated. Charles Spearman continued in the tradition of his predecessors and set the stage for the subsequent development and popularization of factor analysis in the early 20th century. It is noteworthy that many of the early contributors to formal measurement (including Alfred Binet, who developed tests of mental ability in France in the early 1900s) shared an interest in intellectual abilities. Hence much of the early work in psychometrics was applied to "mental testing."

The role of psychophysics. Another historical root of modern psychometrics arose from psychophysics. Attempts to apply the measurement procedures of physics to the study of sensations led to a protracted debate regarding the nature of measurement. Narens and Luce (1986) have summarized the issues. They note that in the late 19th century, Helmholtz observed that physical attributes, such as length and mass, possessed the same intrinsic mathematical structure as did positive real numbers. For example, units of length or mass could be ordered and added as could ordinary numbers. In the early 1900s, the debate continued. The Commission of the British Association for Advancement of Science regarded fundamental measurement of psychological variables to be impossible because of the problems inherent in ordering or adding sensory perceptions. S. S. Stevens argued that strict additivity, as would apply to length or mass, was not necessary and pointed out that individuals could make fairly consistent ratio judgments of sound intensity. For example, they could judge one sound to be twice or half as loud as another. He argued that this ratio property enabled the data from such measurements to be subjected to mathematical manipulation. Stevens is credited with classifying measurements into nominal, ordinal, interval, and ratio scales. Loudness judgments, he argued, conformed to a ratio scale (Duncan, 1984). At about the time that Stevens was presenting his arguments on the legitimacy of scaling psychophysical measures, L. L. Thurstone was developing the mathematical foundations of factor analysis (Nunnally, 1978). Thurstone's interests spanned both psychophysics and mental abilities. According to Duncan (1984), Stevens credited Thurstone with applying psychophysical methods to the scaling of social stimuli. Thus his work represents a convergence of what had been separate historical roots.

CONTEMPORARY DEVELOPMENTS IN MEASUREMENT

Evolution of basic concepts. As influential as Stevens has been, his conceptualization of measurement is by no means the final word. He defined measurement as the "assignment of numerals to objects or events according to rules" (Duncan, 1984). Duncan (1984) challenged this definition as "incomplete in the same way that 'playing the piano is striking the keys of the instrument according to some pattern' is incomplete. Measurement is not only the assignment of numerals, etc. It is also the assignment of numerals in such a way as to correspond to *different degrees of a quality* [original emphasis] . . . or property of some object or event" (p. 126). Narens and Luce (1986) also identified limitations in Stevens's original conceptualization of measurement and illustrated a number of subsequent refinements. However, their work underscores a basic point of Stevens: Measurement models other than the type endorsed by the Commission (of the British Association for Advancement of Science) exist, and these lead to measurement methods applicable to the nonphysical as well as physical sciences. In essence, this work on the fundamental properties of measures has established the scientific legitimacy of the types of measurement procedures used in the social sciences.

Evolution of "mental testing." Although, traditionally, "mental testing" (or "ability testing" as it is now more commonly known) has been an active area of psychometrics, it is not a primary focus of this volume. Many of the advances in that branch of psychometrics are less common and, arguably, less warranted when the goal is to measure characteristics other than abilities. These advances include *item-response theory,* and the use of *logistic models* to describe how individual items relate to the construct of interest (see Crocker and Algina, 1986, for a more extensive introduction to these topics or, for a detailed treatment, Lord and Novick, 1968). Although I will refer in passing to some of these advances associated primarily with standardized ability or achievement testing, I will emphasize the "classical" methods that continue to dominate the measurement of social and psychological phenomena other than abilities.

Broadening the domain of psychometrics. Duncan (1984) notes that the impact of psychometrics in the social sciences has transcended its origins in the measurement of sensations and intellectual abilities. Psychometrics has emerged as a methodological paradigm in its own right. Duncan supports this argument with three examples of the impact of psychometrics: (1) the widespread use of psychometric definitions of reliability and validity, (2) the popularity of factor analysis in social science research, and (3) the adoption of psychometric methods for developing scales measuring an array of variables far broader than those with which psychometrics was initially concerned (p. 203). The applicability of psychometric concepts and methods to the measurement of diverse psychological and social phenomena will occupy our attention for the remainder of this volume.

THE ROLE OF MEASUREMENT
IN THE SOCIAL SCIENCES

The relationship of theory to measurement. The phenomena we try to measure in social science research often derive from theory. Consequently, theory plays a key role in how we conceptualize our measurement problems. Of course, many areas of science measure things derived from theory. Until a subatomic particle is confirmed through measurement, it too is merely a theoretical construct. However, theory in psychology and other social sciences is different from theory in the physical sciences. Social scientists tend to rely on numerous theoretical models that concern rather narrowly circumscribed phenomena whereas theories in the physical sciences are fewer in number and more comprehensive in scope. Festinger's (1954) social comparison theory, for example, focuses on a rather narrow range of human experience: the way people evaluate their own abilities or opinions by comparing themselves to others. In contrast, physicists continue to work toward a unified field theory that will embrace all of the fundamental forces of nature within a single conceptual framework. Also, the social sciences are less mature than physical sciences and their theories are evolving more rapidly. Measuring elusive, intangible phenomena derived from multiple, evolving theories poses a clear challenge to social science researchers. Therefore, it is especially important to be mindful of measurement procedures and to recognize fully their strengths and shortcomings.

The more researchers know about the phenomena in which they are interested, the abstract relationships that exist among hypothetical constructs, and the quantitative tools available to them, the better equipped they are to develop reliable, valid, and usable scales. Knowledge of the specific phenomenon of interest is probably the most important of these considerations. For example, social comparison theory has many aspects that may imply different measurement strategies. Thus one research question might require operationalizing social comparisons as relative preference for information about higher- or lower-status others, while another might dictate ratings of self relative to the "typical person" on various dimensions. Developing a measure that is optimally suited to the research question requires understanding the subtleties of the theory.

Many—arguably, most—of the variables of interest to social and behavioral scientists are not directly observable, of which beliefs, motivational states, expectancies, needs, emotions, and social role perceptions are but a few examples. Some variables, such as gender or age, are essentially self-evident or can be accurately determined by means of existing records. Other variables cannot be directly observed but can be determined by research procedures other than questionnaires. For example, although cognitive researchers cannot directly observe how individuals organize information about gender into their self schemas, they may be able to use recall procedures to make inferences about how individuals structure their thoughts about self and gender. There are many instances in which it is impossible or impractical to assess social science variables with any method other than a paper-and-pencil measurement scale. This is often, but not always, the case when we are interested in measuring theoretical constructs. Thus, an investigator interested in measuring androgyny may find it far easier to do so by means of a carefully developed questionnaire than by some alternative procedure.

Theoretical and atheoretical measures. At this point, we should acknowledge that although this book focuses on measures of theoretical constructs, not all paper-and-pencil measures need be theoretical. Sex and age, for example, can be ascertained from self-report by means of a questionnaire. Even when a variable of interest is not easily observed or validated, there may be times when it is useful to generate items atheoretically and determine how things sort out purely on empirical grounds. For example, a market researcher might ask parents to list the types of toys they have bought for their children and then might explore these listings for patterns of relationships. Usually, this type of purely empirical approach is most useful when an investigator is in the process of developing a theory or model rather than testing or applying it. Thus the market researcher might use the observed patterns of toy purchases as the basis for developing a model of purchasing behavior.

Other examples of relatively atheoretical measurement are public opinion questionnaires and certain ability tests. Asking people which brand of soap they use or for whom they intend to vote seldom involves any attempt to tap an underlying theoretical construct. Rather, the interest is in the subject's response per se, not in some characteristic of the person it is presumed to reflect. Similarly, ability tests can and have been used to develop theories of intelligence or aptitude but are more often used in an applied context to quantify ability or performance relative to some normative standard.

Distinguishing between theoretical and atheoretical measurement situations can be difficult at times. For example, seeking a voter's preference in presidential candidates as a means of predicting the outcome of an election amounts to asking a respondent to report his or her behavioral intention. The relationship of this intention to the event of interest, namely actual voting behavior, is fairly straightforward if not entirely atheoretical. If, on the other hand, the same question is asked in order to determine how conservative or liberal the voter is, the investigator probably has at least an implicit theory relating liberalism–conservatism to candidate preference. The information about voting is not intended to reveal how the respondent will vote but to shed light on some individual characteristic. In these two instances the relevance or irrelevance of the measure to theory is a matter of the investigator's intent, not the procedures used. Readers interested in learning more about constructing survey questionnaires that are not primarily concerned with measuring hypothetical constructs are referred to Converse and Presser (1986) and other volumes in the Applied Social Research Methods series, namely by Fowler (1988), Fowler and Mangione (1989) and Lavrakas (1987).

Measurement scales. Measurement instruments that are collections of items intended to reveal levels of theoretical variables, not readily observable by direct means, are usually referred to as *scales*. We develop scales when we want to measure phenomena that we believe to exist because of our theoretical understanding of the world, but which we cannot assess directly. For example, we may invoke depression or anxiety as explanations for behaviors we observe. Most theoreticians would agree that depression or anxiety is not equivalent to the behavior we see, but underlies it. Our theories suggest that these phenomena exist and that they influence behavior, but that they are intangible. Sometimes, it may be appropriate to infer their existence from their behavioral consequences. However, at other times, we may not have access to behavioral information (as when we are restricted to mail survey methodologies), may not be sure how to interpret available samples of behavior (as when a person remains passive in the face of an event that most others would react to strongly), or are unwilling to assume that behavior is isomorphic with the underlying construct of interest (as when we suspect that crying is the result of joy rather than sadness). In instances when we cannot rely on behavior as an indication of a phenomenon, it may be more useful to assess the construct by means of a carefully constructed and validated scale.

A scale should be contrasted to an *index*. As the terms are used in this volume, a scale consists of what Bollen (1989, pp. 64-65) terms "effect indicators"—that is, items whose values are caused by an underlying construct (or "latent variable," as we shall refer to it in the next chapter). An index, on the other hand, is made up of "cause indicators," or items that determine the level of a construct. For a *scale* measuring an underlying construct, like optimism, responses to items presumably are caused by the construct more optimism causes higher item scores. In contrast, for a socioeconomic status (SES) *index* based partly on education, for example, having more education is not caused by higher SES; it influences SES.

All scales are not created equal. Regrettably, not all scales are developed carefully. Researchers often "throw together" or "dredge up" items and assume they constitute a suitable scale. A researcher not only may fail to exploit theory in developing a scale, but also may reach erroneous conclusions about a theory by misinterpreting what a scale measures. An unfortunate but distressingly common occurrence is the conclusion that some *construct* is unimportant or that some *theory* is inconsistent, based on the performance of a *measure* that may not reflect the variable assumed by the investigator. Consider a hypothetical situation in which an investigator wishes to perform a secondary analysis on an existing data set. Let us assume that our investigator is interested in the role of social support on subsequent professional attainment. The investigator observes that the available data set contains a wealth of information on subjects' professional status over an extended period of time and that subjects were asked whether they were married. In fact, there may be several items, collected at various times, that pertain to marriage. Let us further assume that, in the absence of any data providing a more detailed assessment of social support, the investigator decides to sum these marriage items into a "scale" and to use this as a measure of support.

Although this situation is hypothetical, one actually can find published examples of researchers making judgments about the role of social support on the basis of marital status or equally questionable indicators (see Wallston, Alagna, DeVellis, & DeVellis, 1983, for a review). Equating social support with marital status is not justified. The latter both omits important aspects of social support (e.g., the perceived quality of support received) and includes potentially irrelevant factors (e.g., status as a child versus adult at the time of measurement).

Costs of poor measurement. Even if a poor measure is the only one available, the costs of using it may be greater than any benefits attained. It is rare in the social sciences that there are situations in which an immediate decision must be made in order to avoid dire consequences and one has no other choice but to make do with the best instruments available. Even in these rare instances, however, the inherent problems of using poor measures to assess constructs do not vanish. Does this mean that we should only use measurement tools that have undergone rigorous development and extensive validation testing? Although imperfect measurement may be better than no measurement at all in some situations, we should *recognize* when our measurement procedures are flawed and temper our conclusions accordingly.

Often, an investigator will consider measurement as secondary to more important scientific issues that motivate a study and attempt to "economize" by skimping on measurement. However, adequate measures are a necessary condition for valid research. Investigators should strive for an isomorphism between the theoretical constructs in which they have an interest and the methods of measurement they use to operationalize them. Poor measurement imposes an absolute limit on the validity of the conclusions one can reach. For an investigator who prefers to pay as little attention to measurement and as much to substantive issues as possible, an appropriate strategy might be to get the measurement part of the investigation correct from the very beginning so that it can be taken more or less for granted thereafter.

A researcher also can falsely economize by using scales that are too brief in the hope of reducing the burden to respondents. Choosing a questionnaire that is too brief to be reliable is a bad idea no matter how much respondents prefer its brevity. A reliable questionnaire that is completed by half of the respondents yields more information than an unreliable questionnaire, completed by all respondents, but so prone to error as to be uninterpretable. If you cannot determine what the data mean, the amount of information collected is irrelevant.

SUMMARY AND PREVIEW

This chapter has stressed that measurement is a fundamental activity in all branches of science, including the behavioral and social sciences. Psychometrics, the specialty area of the social sciences that is concerned with measuring social and psychological phenomena, has historical antecedents extending back to ancient times. In the social sciences, theory plays a vital role in the development of measurement scales, which are collections of items that reveal the level of an underlying theoretical variable. However, not all collections of items constitute scales in this sense. Developing scales may be more demanding than selecting items casually; however, the costs of using "informal" measures usually greatly outweigh the benefits.

The following chapters cover the rationale and methods of scale development in greater detail. Chapter 2 explores the "latent variable," the underlying construct that a scale attempts to quantify, and presents the theoretical bases for the methods described in later chapters. Chapter 3 provides a conceptual foundation for understanding reliability and the logic underlying the reliability coefficient. The fourth chapter reviews validity, while the fifth is a practical guide to the steps involved in scale development. Chapter 6 introduces factor analytic concepts and describes their use in scale development. Finally, Chapter 7 briefly discusses how scales fit into the broader research process.

2

Understanding the "Latent Variable"

This chapter presents a conceptual schema for understanding the relationship between measures and the constructs they represent, though it is not the only framework available. For example, latent-trait models (e.g., Crocker & Algina, 1986), although often used in developing ability tests, will be reviewed only briefly. Because of its relative conceptual and computational accessibility and wide usage, I emphasize the classical measurement model, which assumes that individual items are comparable indicators of the underlying construct.

CONSTRUCTS VERSUS MEASURES

Typically, researchers are interested in constructs rather than items or scales per se. For example, a market researcher measuring parents' aspirations for their children would be more interested in intangible parental sentiments and hopes about what their children will accomplish than in where those parents place marks on a questionnaire. However, recording responses to a questionnaire may, in many cases, be the best method of assessing those sentiments and hopes. Scale items are usually a means to the end of construct assessment. In other words, they are necessary because many constructs cannot be assessed directly.

The underlying phenomenon or construct that a scale is intended to reflect is often called the *latent variable*. Exactly what is a latent variable? Its name reveals two chief features. Consider the example of parents' aspirations for children's achievement. First, it is *latent* rather than manifest. Parents' aspirations for their children's achievement are not directly observable. In addition, the construct is *variable* rather than constant—that is, some aspect of it, such as its strength or magnitude, changes. Parents' aspirations for their children's achievement may vary over time (e.g., during the child's infancy versus adolescence), place (e.g, on an athletic field versus a classroom), people (e.g., parents whose own backgrounds or careers differ), or any combination of these and other dimensions. The latent variable is the actual phenomenon that is of interest, in this case, child achievement aspirations. Although we cannot observe or quantify it directly, the latent variable presumably takes on a specific value under some specified set of conditions. A scale developed to measure a latent variable is intended to estimate its actual magnitude at the time and place of measurement for each person measured. This unobservable "actual magnitude" is the *true score*.

LATENT VARIABLE AS THE PRESUMED CAUSE OF ITEM VALUES

The notion of a latent variable implies a certain relationship between it and the items that tap it. The latent variable is regarded as a *cause* of the item score—that is, the strength or quantity of the latent variable (i.e., the value of its true score) is presumed to cause an item (or set of items) to take on a certain value.

An example may reinforce this point: The following are hypothetical items for assessing parents' aspirations for children's achievement:

1. My child's achievements determine my own success.
2. I will do almost anything to ensure my child's success.
3. No sacrifice is too great if it helps my child achieve success.
4. My child's accomplishments are more important to me than just about anything else I can think of.

If parents were given an opportunity to express how strongly they agree with each of these items, their underlying aspirations for childhood achievement should influence their responses. In other words, each item should give an indication of how strong the latent variable, aspirations for children's achievement, is. The score obtained on the item is caused by the strength or quantity of the latent variable for that person, at that particular time.

A causal relationship between a latent variable and a measure implies certain empirical relationships. For example, if an item value is caused by a latent variable, then there should be a correlation between that value and the true score of the latent variable. Because we cannot directly assess the true score, we cannot compute a correlation between it and the item. However, when we examine a set of items that are presumably caused by the same latent variable, we can examine their relationships to one another. So, if we had several items like the ones above measuring parental aspirations for child achievement, we could look directly at how they correlated with one another, invoke the latent variable as the basis for the correlations among items, and use that information to infer how highly each item was correlated with the latent variable.

Shortly, I will explain how all this can be learned from correlations among items. First, however, I will introduce some diagrammatic procedures to help make this explanation more clear.

PATH DIAGRAMS

Coverage of this topic will be limited to issues pertinent to scale development. For greater depth, consult Asher (1983), Duncan (1975), or Kenny (1979).

Diagrammatic conventions. Path diagrams are a method for depicting *causal* relationships among variables. Although they can be used in conjunction with path analysis, which is a data analytic method, path diagrams have more general utility as a means of specifying how a set of variables are interrelated.

These diagrams adhere to certain conventions. A *straight arrow* drawn from one variable label to another indicates that the two are *causally related* and that the direction of causality is as indicated by the arrow. Thus $X \rightarrow Y$ indicates explicitly that X is the cause of Y. Often, associational paths are identified by labels, such as the letter "*a*" in this example:

$$X \longrightarrow a \longrightarrow Y$$

The *absence* of an arrow also has an explicit meaning, namely that two variables are *unrelated.* Thus:

$$A \longrightarrow B \longrightarrow C \qquad D \longrightarrow E$$

specifies that A causes B, B causes C, C and D are *unrelated,* and D causes E.

Another convention of path diagrams is the method of representing *error,* which is usually depicted as an additional causal variable. This error term is a *residual,* representing all sources of variation not accounted for by other causes explicitly depicted in the diagram.

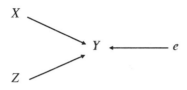

Because this error term is a residual, it represents the discrepancy between the actual value of Y and what we would predict Y to be, based on knowledge of X and Z (in this case). Sometimes, the error term is assumed and thus not included in the diagram (see the following example).

   Path diagrams in scale development. Path diagrams can help us see how scale items are causally related to a latent variable. They can also help us understand how certain relationships among items imply certain relationships between items and the latent variable. We begin by examining a simple computational rule for path diagrams. Let us look at a simple path diagram:

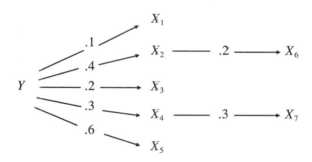

The numbers along the paths are *standardized path coefficients.* Each one expresses the strength of the causal relationship between the variables joined by the arrow. The fact that the coefficients are standardized means that they all use the same scale to quantify the causal relationships. In this diagram, Y is a cause of X_1 through X_5. A useful relationship exists between the values of path coefficients and the correlations between the Xs (which would represent items, in the case of a scale development-type path diagram). For diagrams like this one having only one common origin (Y, in this case), the correlation between any two Xs is equal to the product of the coefficients for the arrows forming a route, through Y, between the X variables in question. For example, the correlation between X_1 and X_5 is calculated by multiplying the two standardized path coefficients that join them via Y. Thus, $r_{15} = .6 \times .1 = .06$. Variables X_6 and X_7 also share Y as a common source, but the route connecting them is longer. However, the rule still applies. Beginning at X_7, we can trace back to Y and then forward again to X_6. (Or, we could have gone in the other direction, from X_6 to X_7.) The result is: $.3 \times .3 \times .4 \times .2 = .0072$. Thus, $r_{67} = .0072$.

This relationship between path coefficients and correlations provides a basis for estimating paths between a latent variable and the items that it influences. Even though the latent variable is hypothetical and unmeasurable, the items are real and the correlations among them can be directly computed. By using these correlations, the simple rule just discussed, and some assumptions about the relationships among items and the true score, we can come up with estimates for the paths between the items and the latent variable. We can begin with a set of correlations among variables. Then, working backwards from the relationship among paths and correlations, we can determine what the values of certain paths must be if the assumptions are correct. Let us consider the following example:

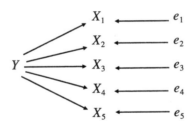

This diagram is similar to the example considered earlier except that there are no path values, the variables X_6 and X_7 have been dropped, the remaining X variables represent scale items, and each item has a variable (error) other than Y influencing it. These e variables are unique in the case of each item and represent the residual variation in each item not explained by Y. This diagram indicates that all of the items are influenced by Y. In addition, each is influenced by a unique set of variables other than Y that are collectively treated as error.

This revised diagram represents how five individual items are related to a single latent variable, Y. The numbers given to the es and Xs indicate that the five items are different and that the five sources of error, one for each item, are also different. The diagram has no arrows going directly from one X to another X or going from an e to another e or from an e to an X other than the one with which it is associated. These aspects of the diagram represent assumptions that will be discussed later.

If we had five actual items that a group of people had completed, we would have item scores that we could then correlate with one another. The rule examined earlier allowed the computations of correlations from path coefficients. With the addition of some assumptions, it also lets us compute path coefficients from correlations—that is, correlations computed from actual items can be used to determine how each item relates to the latent variable. If, for example, X_1 and X_4 have a correlation of .49, then we know that the product of the values for the path leading from Y to X_1 and the path leading from Y to X_4 is equal to .49. We know this because our rule established that the correlation of two variables equals the product of the path coefficients along the route that joins them. If we also assume that the *two path values are equal,* then they both must be .70.[1]

FURTHER ELABORATION OF THE MEASUREMENT MODEL

Classical measurement assumptions. The classical measurement model starts with common assumptions about items and their relationships to the latent variable and sources of error:

1. The amount of error associated with individual items varies randomly. The error associated with individual items has a mean of zero when aggregated across a large number of people. Thus, items' means tend to be unaffected by error when a large number of respondents complete the items.

2. One item's error term is *not* correlated with another item's error term; the only routes linking items pass through the latent variable, never through any error term.

3. Error terms are *not* correlated with the true score of the latent variable. Note that the paths emanating from the latent variable do not extend outward to the error terms. The arrow between an item and its error term aims the other way.

The first two assumptions above are common statistical assumptions that underlie many analytic procedures. The third amounts to defining "error" as the residual remaining after considering all of the relationships between a set of predictors and an outcome, or, in this case, a set of items and their latent variable.

PARALLEL "TESTS"

Classical measurement theory, in its most orthodox form, is based on the assumption of parallel tests. The term *parallel tests* stems from the fact that one can view each individual item as a "test" for the value of the latent variable. For our purposes, referring to parallel items would be more accurate. However, I will defer to convention and use the traditional name.

A virtue of the parallel tests model is that its assumptions make it quite easy to reach useful conclusions about how individual items relate to the latent variable, based on our observations of how the items relate to one another. Earlier, I suggested that, with a knowledge of the correlations among items and with certain assumptions, one could make inferences about the paths leading from a causal variable to an item. As will be shown in the next chapter, being able to assign a numerical value to the relationships between the latent variable and the items themselves is quite important. Thus, in this section, I will examine in some detail how the assumptions of parallel tests lead to certain conclusions that make this possible.

The rationale underlying the model of parallel tests is that each item of a scale is precisely as good a measure of the latent variable as any other of the scale items. The individual items are thus *strictly parallel,* which is to say that each item's relationship to the latent variable is presumed identical to every other item's relationship to that variable *and* the amount of error present in each item is also presumed to be identical.

Diagrammatically, this model can be represented as follows:

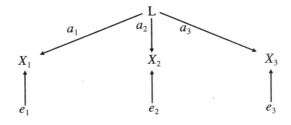

This model adds two assumptions to those listed earlier:

1. The amount of influence from the latent variable to each item is assumed to be the same for all items.

2. Each item is assumed to have the same amount of error as any other item, meaning that the influence of factors other than the latent variable is equal for all items.

These added assumptions mean that the correlation of each item with the true score is identical. Being able to assert that these correlations are *equal* is important because it leads to a means of determining the *value* for each of these identical correlations. This, in turn, leads to a means of quantifying reliability, which will be discussed in the next chapter.

Asserting that correlations between the true score and each item are equal requires *both* of the preceding assumptions. A squared correlation is the proportion of variance shared between two variables. So, if correlations between the true score and each of two items are equal, the proportions of variance shared between the true score and each item also must be equal. Assume that a true score contributes the same *amount* of variance to each of two items. This amount can be an equal *proportion* of total variance for each item only if the items have identical total variances. In order for the total variances to be equal for the two items, the amount of variance each item receives from sources other than the true score must also be equal. As all variation sources other than the true score are lumped together as error, this means that the two items must have equal error variances. For example, if X_1 got 9 arbitrary units of variation from its true score and 1 from error, the true score proportion would be 90% of total variation. If X_2 also got 9 units of variation from the true score, these 9 units could only be 90% of the total if the total variation were 10. The total could only equal 10 if error contributed 1 unit to X_2 as it did to X_1. The correlation between each item and the true score then would equal the square root of the proportion of each item's variance that is attributable to the true score, or .30 in this case.

Thus because the parallel tests model assumes that the amount of influence from the latent variable is the same for each item *and* that the amount from other sources (error) is the same for each item, the proportions of item variance attributable to the latent variable and to error are equal for all items. This also means that, under the assumptions of parallel tests, standardized path coefficients from the latent variable to each item are equal for all items. It was assuming that standardized path coefficients were equal that made it possible, in an earlier example, to compute path coefficients from correlations between items. The path diagram rule, discussed earlier, relating path coefficients to correlations, should help us to understand why these equalities hold when one accepts the preceding assumptions.

The assumptions of this model also imply that correlations among items are identical (e.g., the correlation between X_1 and X_2 is identical to the correlation between X_1 and X_3 or X_2 and X_3). How do we arrive at this conclusion from the assumptions? The correlations are all the same because the only mechanism to account for the correlation between any two items is the route through the latent variable that links those items. For example, X_1 and X_2 are linked only by the route made up of paths a_1 and a_2. The correlation can be computed by tracing the route joining the two items in question and multiplying the path values. For any two items, this entails multiplying two paths that have identical values (i.e., $a_1 = a_2 = a_3$). Correlations computed by multiplying equal values will, of course, be equal.

The assumptions also imply that each of these correlations between items equals the square of any path from the latent variable to an individual item. How do we reach this conclusion? The product of two different paths, e.g., a_1 and a_2, is identical to the square of either path because both path coefficients are identical. If $a_1 = a_2 = a_3$, and $(a_1 \times a_2) = (a_1 \times a_3) = (a_2 \times a_3)$, then each of these latter products must also equal the value of any of the a-paths multiplied by itself.

It also follows from the assumptions of this model that the proportion of error associated with each item is the complement of the proportion of variance that is related to the latent variable. In other words, whatever effect on a given item that is not explained by the latent variable must be explained by error. Together, these two effects explain 100% of the variation in any given item. This is so simply because the error term, e, is defined as encompassing all sources of variation in the item other than the latent variable.

These assumptions support at least one other conclusion: Because each item is influenced equally by the latent variable and each error term's influence on its corresponding item is also equal, the items all have equal means and equal variances. If the only two sources that can influence the mean are identical for all items, then clearly the means for the items also will be identical. This reasoning also holds for the item variances.

In conclusion, the parallel tests model assumes:

1. random error
2. errors not correlated with each other
3. errors not correlated with true score
4. latent variable effects all items equally
5. amount of error for each item is equal

These assumptions allow us to reach a variety of interesting conclusions. Furthermore, the model enables us to make inferences about the latent variable, based on the items' correlations with one another. However, the model accomplishes this feat by setting forth fairly stringent assumptions.

ALTERNATIVE MODELS

As it happens, all of the narrowly restrictive assumptions associated with strictly parallel tests are not necessary in order to make useful inferences about the relationship of true scores to observed scores. A model based on what are technically called *essentially tau-equivalent tests* (or, occasionally, *randomly parallel tests*) makes a more liberal assumption, namely, that the amount of error variance associated with a given item need not equal the error variance of the other items (e.g., Allen & Yen, 1979). Consequently, the *standardized* values of the paths from the latent variable to each item may not be equal. However, the *unstandardized* values of the path from the latent variable to each item (i.e., the *amount* as opposed to *proportion* of influence that the latent variable has on each item) are still presumed to be identical for all items. This means that items are parallel with respect to how much they are influenced by the latent variable but are not necessarily influenced to exactly the same extent by extraneous factors that are lumped together as error. Under strictly parallel assumptions, different items not only tap the true score to the same degree, but their error components are also the same. Tau-equivalency ("tau" is the Greek equivalent to "*t*," as in true score) is much easier to live with because it does not impose the "equal errors" condition. Because errors may vary, item means and variances may also vary. The more liberal assumptions of this model are attractive because finding equivalent measures of equal variance is rare. This model allows us to reach many of the same conclusions as with strictly parallel tests but with less restrictive assumptions. Readers may wish to compare this model to Nunnally's (1978) discussion of the "domain sampling model."

Some scale developers consider even the essentially tau-equivalent model too restrictive. After all, how often can we assume that each item is influenced by the latent variable to the same degree? Tests developed under what is called the *congeneric model* (Jöreskog, 1971) are subject to an even more relaxed set of assumptions (see Carmines & McIver, 1981, for a discussion of congeneric tests). It assumes (beyond the basic measurement assumptions) merely that all the items share a common latent variable. They need not bear equally strong relationships to the latent variable, and their error variances need not be equal. One must assume only that each item reflects the true score to some degree. Of course, the more strongly each item correlates with the true score, the more reliable the scale will be.

An even more liberal approach is the *general factor model*, which allows multiple latent variables to underlie a given set of items. Carmines and McIver (1981) and Long (1983) have discussed the merits of this very general model; chief among them being its improved correspondence to real world data.

The congeneric model is a special case of the factor model (i.e., a single-factor case). Likewise, an essentially tau-equivalent measure is a special case of a congeneric measure—one for which the relationships of items to their latent variable are assumed to be equal. Finally, a strictly parallel test is a special case of an essentially tau-equivalent one, adding the assumption of equal relationships between each item and its associated sources of error.

One other measurement strategy should be mentioned briefly. This is item response theory (IRT), which is also known as latent-trait or strong true score theory. This approach is used primarily, but not exclusively, with dichotomous-response (e.g., correct versus incorrect) items in developing achievement tests. Different models within the broader class of IRTs may be based on the normal or, with increasing frequency, the logistic probability function. IRT assumes that each individual item has its own characteristic sensitivity to the latent variable, represented by an item-characteristic curve (ICC). An ICC is a plot of the relationship between the value of the latent variable (e.g., ability) and the probability of a certain response to an item (e.g., answering it correctly). Thus the curve reveals how much ability an item demands to be answered correctly. Item response theory allows individual items to be calibrated in a way that permits ability assessments across respondents and across tests. IRT shares some of the advantages and disadvantages of Thurstone scales, which are considered briefly in Chapter 5. Readers wishing to learn more about item response theory should consult texts dealing with educational measurement, such as those by Allen and Yen (1979) or Crocker and Algina (1986). For a more detailed account, see Reiser (1981) or Lord and Novick (1968).

Except for a discussion of factor analysis in Chapter 6, we will focus almost exclusively on parallel and essentially tau-equivalent models for several reasons. First, they exemplify "classical" measurement theory. Additionally, discussing the mechanisms by which other models operate can quickly become burdensome. This volume does not assume the facility with statistical concepts that such a discussion would require. Also, many social scientists who are not measurement specialists are unfamiliar with the software needed to use such procedures as IRT. Finally, classical models have proven very useful for social scientists with primary interests other than measurement who, nonetheless, take careful measurement seriously. This group is the audience for whom the present text has been written. For these individuals, the scale development procedures that follow from a classical model generally yield very satisfactory scales. Indeed, although no tally is readily available to my knowledge, I suspect that (outside of ability testing) a substantial majority of the well-known and highly regarded scales used in social science research were developed using such procedures.

EXERCISES

1. How can we infer the relationship between the latent variable and two items related to it, based on the correlations between the two items?
2. What is the chief difference in assumptions between the parallel tests and essentially tau-equivalent models?
3. Which measurement model assumes, beyond the basic assumptions common to all measurement approaches, only that the items share a common latent variable?

NOTE

1. Although −.70 is also an allowable square root of .49, deciding between the positive or negative root is typically of less concern than one would think. As long as all the items can be made to correlate positively with one another (if necessary, by "reverse scoring" certain items as discussed in Chapter 5), then the signs of the path coefficients from the latent variable to the individual items will be the same and are arbitrary. Note, however, that giving positive signs to these paths implies that the items indicate more of the construct whereas negative coefficients would imply the opposite.

3

Reliability

Ghiselli, Campbell, and Zedeck (1981) consider reliability the fundamental issue in psychological measurement (p. 184). Its importance is clear once its meaning is fully understood. Scale reliability is the proportion of variance attributable to the true score of the latent variable. There are several methods for computing reliability but all share this fundamental definition. However, how one conceptualizes and operationalizes reliability differs by computational method.

CONTINUOUS VERSUS DICHOTOMOUS ITEMS

Although items may have a variety of response formats, we assume in this chapter that item responses consist of multiple-value response options. Dichotomous items (i.e., items having only two response options, such as "yes" and "no" or those having multiple response options that can be classified as "right" versus "wrong") are widely used in ability testing and, to a lesser degree, in other measurement contexts. Examples are:

1. Zurich is the capital of Switzerland.   True _____   False _____
2. What is the value of pi?   (a) 1.41   (b) 3.14   (c) 2.78

Special methods for computing reliability that take advantage of the computational simplicity of dichotomous responses have been developed. General measurement texts such as Nunnally (1978) and Crocker and Algina (1986) cover these methods in some detail. The logic of these methods for assessing reliability largely parallels the more general approach that applies to multi-point, continuous scale items. In the interest of brevity, this chapter will make only passing reference to reliability assessment methods intended for scales made up of dichotomous items. Some characteristics of this type of scale are discussed in Chapter 5.

INTERNAL CONSISTENCY

Internal consistency reliability, as the name implies, is concerned with the homogeneity of the items comprising a scale. Scales based on classical measurement models are intended to measure a single phenomenon. As we saw in the preceding chapter, measurement theory suggests that the relationships among items are logically connected to the relationships of items to the latent variable. If the items of a scale have a strong relationship to their latent variable, they will have a strong relationship to each other. Although we cannot directly observe the linkage between items and the latent variable, we can certainly determine whether the items are correlated to one another. A scale is *internally consistent* to the extent that its items are highly intercorrelated. High inter-item correlations suggest that the items are all measuring the same thing. If we make the assumptions discussed in the preceding chapter, we also can conclude that strong correlations among items imply strong links between items and the latent variable. Thus, a unidimensional scale or a single dimension of a multidimensional scale should consist of a set of items that correlate well with each other. Multidimensional scales measuring several phenomena—e.g., the Multidimensional Health Locus of Control (MHLC) scales (Wallston, Wallston, & DeVellis, 1978)—are really families of related scales; each "dimension" is a scale in its own right.

Coefficient alpha. Internal consistency is typically equated with Cronbach's (1951) coefficient alpha, α. We will examine alpha in some detail for several reasons. First, it is widely used as a measure of reliability. Second, its connection to the definition of reliability may be less self-evident than is the case for other measures of reliability (such as the alternate forms methods) discussed later. Consequently, alpha may appear more mysterious than other reliability computation methods to those who are not familiar with its internal workings. Finally, an exploration of the logic underlying the computation of alpha provides a sound basis for comparing how other computational methods capture the essence of what we mean by reliability.

The Kuder-Richardson formula 20, or *KR-20*, as it is more commonly known, is a special version of alpha for items that are dichotomous (e.g., Nunnally, 1978). However, as noted earlier, we will concentrate on the more general form that applies to items having multiple response options.

You can think about all the variability in a set of item scores as due to one two things: (a) actual variation across individuals in the phenomenon that the scale measures (i.e., true variation in the latent variable) and (b) error. This is true because classical measurement models define "the phenomenon" (e.g., patients' desire for control of interactions with a physician) as the source of all shared variation and "error" as any remaining, or unshared, variation in scale scores (e.g., a single item's unintended double meaning). Another way to think about this is to regard total variation as having two components: "signal" (i.e., true differences in patients' desire for control) and "noise" (i.e., score differences caused by everything *but* true differences in desire for control). Computing alpha, as we shall see, partitions the total variance among the set of items into signal and noise components. The proportion of total variation that is signal equals alpha. Thus another way to think about alpha is that it equals 1 − error variance, or, conversely, that error variance = 1 − alpha.

The covariance matrix. To understand internal consistency more fully, it helps to examine the *covariance matrix* of a set of scale items. A covariance matrix for a set of scale items reveals important information about the scale as a whole.

A covariance matrix is a more general form of a correlation matrix. It differs from a correlation matrix in that the data entries are *unstandardized;* that is, it contains the same information, in unstandardized form, as a correlation matrix. The diagonal elements of a covariance matrix are *variances*—covariances of items with themselves—just as the unities along the main diagonal of a correlation matrix are variables' correlations with themselves. Its off-diagonal values are *covariances,* expressing relationships between pairs of unstandardized variables just as correlation coefficients do with standardization. So, conceptually, a covariance matrix consists of (a) variances (on the diagonal) for individual variables and (b) covariances (off-diagonal) representing the unstandardized relationship between variable pairs.

A typical covariance matrix for three variables X_1, X_2, and X_3 is:

	X_1	X_2	X_3
X_1	Var_1	$Cov_{1\,2}$	$Cov_{1\,3}$
X_2	$Cov_{1\,2}$	Var_2	$Cov_{2\,3}$
X_3	$Cov_{1\,3}$	$Cov_{2\,3}$	Var_3

or, somewhat more compactly using the customary symbols for matrices, variances, and covariances,

$$\begin{bmatrix} \sigma_1^2 & \sigma_{1\,2} & \sigma_{1\,3} \\ \sigma_{1\,2} & \sigma_2^2 & \sigma_{2\,3} \\ \sigma_{1\,3} & \sigma_{2\,3} & \sigma_3^2 \end{bmatrix}$$

Covariance matrices for multi-item scales. Let us focus our attention on the properties of a covariance matrix for a set of items that, when added together, make up a scale. The covariance matrix presented above has three variables, X_1, X_2, and X_3. Assume that these variables are actually scores for three items and that the items, X_1, X_2, and X_3, when added together make up a scale we will call Y. What can this matrix tell us about the relationship of the individual items to the scale as a whole?

A covariance matrix has a number of very interesting (well, useful, at least) properties. Among these is the fact that adding all of the elements in the matrix together (i.e., summing the variances, which are along the diagonal and the covariances, which are off of the diagonal) gives a value that is exactly equal to the variance of the scale as a whole, assuming that the items are equally weighted. So, if we add all the terms in the symbolic covariance matrix, the resulting sum would be the variance of scale Y. This is very important and bears repeating: The variance of a scale, Y, made up of any number of items, equals the sum of all the values in the covariance matrix for those items, assuming equal item weighting.[1] Thus the variance of a scale Y, made up of three equally weighted items, X_1, X_2, and X_3, has the following relationship to the covariance matrix of the items: $\sigma_y^2 = C$, where,

$$C = \begin{bmatrix} \sigma_1^2 & \sigma_{1\,2} & \sigma_{1\,3} \\ \sigma_{1\,2} & \sigma_2^2 & \sigma_{2\,3} \\ \sigma_{1\,3} & \sigma_{2\,3} & \sigma_3^2 \end{bmatrix}$$

Readers who would like more information about the topics covered in this section are referred to Nunnally (1978) for covariance matrices, and Namboodiri (1984) for an introduction to matrix algebra in statistics. The covariance matrix for the individual items has other useful information. Applications that can be derived from item covariance matrices are discussed by Bohrnstedt (1969).

Alpha and the covariance matrix. Alpha is defined as the proportion of a scale's total variance that is attributable to a common source, presumably the true score of a latent variable underlying the items. Thus if we want to compute alpha, it would be useful to have a value for the scale's total variance and a value for the proportion that is "common" variance. The covariance matrix is just what we need in order to do this.

Recall the diagram we used in Chapter 2 to show how items related to their latent variable:

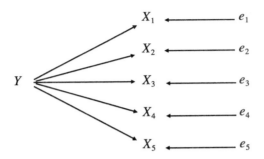

All of the variation in items that is due to the latent variable, Y, is *shared* or *common*. (The terms *joint* and *communal* are also used to describe this variation.) When Y varies (as it will, for example, across individuals having different levels of the attribute it represents), scores on *all* the items will vary with it because it is a cause of those scores. Thus if Y is high, *all* the item scores will tend to be high; if Y is low, they will tend to be low. This means that the items will tend to *vary jointly* (i.e., be correlated with one another). So, the latent variable affects all of the items and thus they are correlated. The error terms, in contrast, are the source of the *unique* variation that each item possesses. Whereas all items share variability due to Y, no two share any variation from the *same* error source, under our classical measurement assumptions. The value of a given error term only affects the score of one item. Thus, the error terms are not correlated with one another. So, each item (and, by implication the scale defined by the sum of the items) varies as a function of: (a) the source of variation common to itself and the other items and (b) unique, unshared variation that we refer to as error. It follows that the total variance for each item, and hence for the scale as a whole, must be a combination of variance from common and unique sources. According to the definition of reliability, alpha should equal the ratio of common-source variation to total variation.

Now, consider a k-item measure called Y whose covariance matrix is as follows:

$$\begin{bmatrix} \sigma_1^2 & \sigma_{1\,2} & \sigma_{1\,3} & \cdots & \sigma_{1\,k} \\ \sigma_{1\,2} & \sigma_2^2 & \sigma_{2\,3} & \cdots & \sigma_{2\,k} \\ \sigma_{1\,3} & \sigma_{2\,3} & \sigma_3^2 & \cdots & \sigma_{3\,k} \\ \cdot & \cdot & \cdot & & \cdot \\ \cdot & \cdot & \cdot & & \cdot \\ \cdot & \cdot & \cdot & & \cdot \\ \sigma_{1\,k} & \sigma_{2\,k} & \sigma_{3\,k} & \cdots & \sigma_k^2 \end{bmatrix}$$

The variance, σ_y^2, of the k-item scale equals the sum of all matrix elements. The entries along the main diagonal are the variances of the individual items represented in the matrix. (The variance of the ith item is signified as σ_i^2.) Therefore, the sum of the elements along the main diagonal, $\Sigma \sigma_i^2$, is the sum of the variances of the individual items. Thus the covariance matrix gives us ready access to two values: (a) the total variance of the scale, σ_y^2, defined as the sum of all elements in the matrix and (b) the sum of the individual item variances, $\Sigma \sigma_i^2$, computed by summing entries along the main diagonal. These two values can be given a conceptual interpretation. The sum of the whole matrix is, by definition, the variance of Y, the scale made up of the individual items. However, this total variance, as we have said, can be partitioned into different parts.

Let us consider how the covariance matrix separates common from unique variance by examining how the elements on the main diagonal of the covariance matrix differ from all the off-diagonal elements. All of the variances (diagonal elements) are single-variable or "variable-with-itself" terms. We noted earlier that these variances can be thought of as covariances of items with themselves. Each variance contains information about only one item. In other words, each represents variation that is *unique* to a single item, not joint variation shared among items. The off-diagonal elements of the covariance matrix all involve pairs of terms, and thus common, or joint, variation between two of the scale's items (covariation). Thus the elements in the covariance matrix (and hence the total variance of Y) consist of covariation ("joint variation," if you will) plus "nonjoint" or *unique* variation. As the covariances—and only the covariances—represent joint variation, all unique variation must be represented in the variances along the main diagonal of the covariance matrix and thus by the term $\Sigma \sigma_i^2$. The total variance, of course, is expressed by

σ_y^2, the sum of all the matrix elements. Thus we can express the ratio of unique or non-joint variation to total variation in Y as:

$$\Sigma \, \sigma_i^2 \, / \, \sigma_y^2$$

It thus follows that we can express the proportion of joint or communal variation as the *complement* of this value as shown:

$$1 - (\,\Sigma \, \sigma_i^2 \, / \, \sigma_y^2\,)$$

Because all the communal variation has the latent variable as its common source, this would seem to be what we are after, given our definition of alpha. We still need one more correction, however. The total number of elements in the covariance matrix is k^2. The number of elements in the matrix that are noncommunal (i.e., those along the main diagonal) is k. The number that are communal (all those not on the diagonal) is $k^2 - k$. The fraction in our last formula thus has a numerator based on k values and a denominator based on k^2 values. To adjust our calculations so that the ratio expresses the relative magnitudes rather than the numbers of terms in the numerator and denominator, we multiply the entire expression representing the proportion of communal variation by values to counteract the differences in numbers of terms summed. To do this, we multiply by $k^2 / (k^2 - k)$, or, equivalently, $k / (k - 1)$. This limits the range of possible values for alpha to between 0.0 and 1.0.

Thus our resulting expression is:

$$\alpha = \frac{k}{k - 1} \left(1 - \frac{\Sigma \, \sigma_i^2}{\sigma_{yi}^2} \right)$$

To summarize, a measure's reliability equals the proportion of total variance among its items that is due to the latent variable and thus is communal. The formula for alpha expresses this by specifying the portion of total variance for the item set that is unique, subtracting this from 1 to determine the proportion that is communal, and multiplying by a correction factor to adjust for the number of elements contributing to the earlier computations.

Alternative formula for alpha. Another common formula for computing alpha is based on correlations rather than covariances. Actually, it uses $\bar{r}$, the *average inter-item correlation*. This formula is:

$$\alpha = \frac{k \bar{r}}{1 + (k - 1) \bar{r}}$$

It follows logically from the covariance-based formula for alpha. Consider the covariance formula in conceptual terms:

$$\alpha = \frac{k}{k - 1} \left(1 - \frac{\text{Sum of item variances}}{\text{Sum of variances and covariances}} \right)$$

Note that the numerator and denominator in the term on the right are sums of individual values. However, the sum of these individual values is identical to the mean of the values multiplied by the number of values involved. (For example, 10 numbers that sum to 50 and 10 times the mean of those numbers [i.e., 5] both equal 50.) Therefore, the numerator of the term on the right must equal k times the average item variance $(\bar{v})$ and the denominator must equal k times the average variance plus $(k^2 - k)$ [or, alternatively, $(k)(k - 1)$] times the average covariance $(\bar{c})$:

$$\alpha = \frac{k}{k - 1} \left(1 - \frac{k \bar{v}}{k \bar{v} + (k)(k - 1) \bar{c}} \right)$$

To remove the "1" from the equation, we can replace it with its equivalent $[k \bar{v} + (k)(k - 1) \bar{c}] / [k \bar{v} + (k)(k - 1) \bar{c}]$, which allows us to consolidate the whole term on the right into a single ratio:

$$\alpha = \frac{k}{k - 1} \left(\frac{k \bar{v} + k(k - 1) \bar{c} - k \bar{v}}{k \bar{v} + (k)(k - 1) \bar{c}} \right)$$

or, equivalently,

$$\alpha = \frac{k}{k - 1} \left(\frac{k(k - 1) \bar{c}}{k [\bar{v} + (k - 1) \bar{c}]} \right)$$

Cross-canceling k from the numerator of the left term and denominator of the right term, while cross-canceling $(k - 1)$ from the numerator of the right term and denominator of the left term, yields the simplified expression:

$$\alpha = \frac{k\,\bar{c}}{\bar{v} + (k-1)\,\bar{c}}$$

Recall that the formula we are striving for involves correlations rather than covariances and thus standardized rather than unstandardized terms. After standardizing, an average of covariances is identical to an average of correlations, and a variance equals 1.0. Consequently, we can replace $\bar{c}$ with the average interitem correlation, $\bar{r}$ and $\bar{v}$ with 1.0. This yields:

$$\frac{k\,\bar{r}}{1 + (k-1)\,\bar{r}}$$

This formula is known as the *Spearman-Brown prophecy formula* (Crocker & Algina, 1986), and one of its important uses will be illustrated in the section of this chapter dealing with split-half reliability computation.

Reliability and statistical power. An often overlooked benefit of more reliable scales is that they increase *statistical power* for a given sample size (or allow a smaller sample size to yield equivalent power), relative to less reliable measures. To have a specified degree of confidence in the ability to detect a difference of a given magnitude between two experimental groups, for example, one needs a particular size sample. The probability of detecting such a difference (i.e., the power of the statistical test) can be increased by increasing the sample size. In many applications, much the same effect can be obtained by improving the reliability of measurement. A reliable measure, like a larger sample, contributes relatively less error to the statistical analysis. Researchers might do well to weigh the relative advantages of increasing scale reliability versus sample size in research situations where both options are available.

The power gains from improving reliability depend on a number of factors, including the initial sample size, the probability level set for detecting a Type I error, the effect size (e.g., mean difference) that is considered significant, and the proportion of error variance that is attributable to measure unreliability rather than sample heterogeneity or other sources. A precise comparison between reliability enhancement and sample size increase requires that these factors be specified; however, the following examples illustrate the point. In a hypothetical research situation with the probability of a Type I error set at .01, a 10-point difference between two means regarded as important, and an error variance equal to

100, the sample size would have to be increased from 128 to 172 (34% increase) to raise the power of an F test from .80 to .90. Reducing the total error variance from 100 to 75 (25% decrease) would have essentially the same result without increasing the sample size. Substituting a highly reliable scale for a substantially poorer one might accomplish this. As another example, for $N = 50$, two scales with reliabilities of .38 that have a correlation ($r = .24$) barely achieving significance at $p < .10$ are significant at $p < .01$ if their reliabilities are increased to .90. If the reliabilities remained at .38, a sample more than twice as large would be needed for the correlation to reach $p < .01$. Lipsey (1990) provides a more comprehensive discussion of statistical power, including the effects of measurement reliability.

RELIABILITY BASED ON CORRELATIONS BETWEEN SCALE SCORES

There are alternatives to internal consistency reliability. These types of reliability computation involve having the same set of people complete two separate versions of a scale or the same version on multiple occasions.

Alternate forms reliability. If two strictly parallel forms of a scale exist, then the correlation between them can be computed as long as the same people complete both parallel forms. For example, assume that a researcher first developed two equivalent sets of items measuring patients' desire for control when interacting with physicians, then administered both sets of items to a group of patients and, finally, correlated the scores from one set of items with the scores from the other set. This correlation would be the alternate forms reliability. Recall that parallel forms are made up of items, all of which (either within or between forms) do an equally good job of measuring the latent variable. This implies that both forms of the scale have identical alphas, means, and variances and measure the same phenomenon. In essence, parallel forms consist of one set of items that have more or less arbitrarily been divided into two subsets that make up the two parallel, alternate forms of the scale. Under these conditions, the correlation between one form and the other is equivalent to correlating either form with itself, as each alternate form is equivalent to the other.

Split-half reliability. A problem with alternate forms reliability is that we usually do not have two versions of a scale that conform strictly to the assumptions of parallel tests. However, there are other reliability estimates that apply the same sort of logic to a single set of items. Because alternate forms are essentially made up of a single pool of items that have been divided in two, it follows that we can (a) take the set of items that make up a single scale (i.e., a scale that does not have any alternate form), (b) divide that set of items into two subsets, and (c) correlate the subsets to assess reliability.

A reliability measure of this type is called a split-half reliability. Split-half reliability is really a class rather than a single type of computational method because there are a variety of ways in which the scale can be split in half. One method is to compare the first half of the items to the second half. This type of *first-half last-half split* may be problematic, however, because factors other than the value of the latent variable (in other words, sources of error) might affect each subset differently. For example, if the items making up the scale in question were scattered throughout a lengthy questionnaire, the respondents might be more fatigued when completing the second half of the scale. *Fatigue* would then differ systematically between the two halves and would thus make them appear less similar. However, the dissimilarity would not be so much a characteristic of the items per se as of their position in the item order of the scale. Other factors that might differentiate earlier-occurring from later-occurring items are a *practice effect* whereby respondents might get better at answering the items as they go along, or *failure to complete* the entire set of items, or possibly even something as mundane as changes in the *print quality* of a questionnaire from front to back. As with fatigue, these factors would lower the correlation between halves because of the order in which the scale items were presented and not because of the quality of the scale items. As a result of factors such as these, measuring the strength of the relationships among items may be complicated by circumstances not directly related to item quality, resulting in an erroneous reliability assessment.

To avoid some of the pitfalls associated with item order, one can assess another type of split-half reliability known as *odd-even reliability.* In this instance, the subset of odd-numbered items is compared to the even-numbered items. This assures that each of the two subsets of items consist of an equal number from each section (i.e., beginning, middle, end) of the original scale. Assuming that item order is irrelevant (as opposed to the "easy-to-hard" order common to achievement tests, for example) this method avoids many of the problems associated with first-half vesus second-half split halves.

In theory, there are many other ways to arrive at split-half reliability. Two alternatives to the methods discussed above for constituting the item subsets are *balanced halves* and *random halves*. In the former case, one would identify some potentially important item characteristics (such as first-person wording, item length, or whether a certain type of response indicates the presence or absence of the attribute in question). The two halves of the scale would then be constituted so as to have the characteristics equally represented in each half. Thus an investigator might divide up the items so that each subset had the same number of items worded in the first-person, the same number of short items, and so on. However, when considering multiple item characteristics, it might be impossible to balance the proportion of one without making it impossible to balance another. This would be the case, for example, if there were more long than short first-person items. Creating a balance for the latter characteristic would necessitate an imbalance of the former. Also, it may be difficult to determine which characteristics of the items should be balanced.

An investigator could obtain random halves merely by randomly allocating each item to one of the two subsets that will eventually be correlated with one another to compute the reliability estimate. How well this works depends on the number of items, the number of characteristics of concern, and the degree of independence among the characteristics. Hoping that a small number of items, varying along several interrelated dimensions, will yield comparable groupings through randomization is unrealistic. On the other hand, randomly assigning a set of 50 items varying with respect to two or three uncorrelated characteristics to two categories might yield reasonably comparable subsets.

Which method of achieving split halves is best depends on the particular situation. What is most important is that the investigator think about how dividing the items might result in nonequivalent subsets and what steps can be taken to avoid this. The reasoning behind both split-halves and alternate-forms reliability is a natural extension of the parallel tests model.

Although when we initially discussed that model, we regarded each item as a "test," one can also regard a scale (or the two halves of a scale) that conforms to the model as a "test." Therefore, we can apply the logic we used in the case of several items to the case of two alternate forms or two halves of a scale. Consider two "tests" (scale halves or alternate forms) under the parallel tests assumptions:

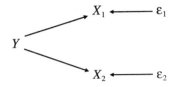

The only route linking the two consists of the causal paths from the latent variable to each. Thus the product of these paths' values equals the correlation between the tests. If the path values have to be equal (and they do, under the assumptions of this model), then the correlation between the tests equals the square of the path value from latent variable to either test. The square of that path (assuming that it is a standardized path coefficient) is also the proportion of variance in either test that is influenced by the latent variable. This, in turn, is the definition of reliability. Thus the correlation between the two tests equals the reliability of each.

Whereas the "tests" referred to in the preceding paragraph are two complete versions of a scale in the alternate forms case, they are two half-scales in the split-half instance. Thus the correlation between two split-halves yields a reliability estimate for each *half* of the whole set of items, which is an underestimate of the reliability for the entire set. An estimate of the reliability of the entire scale, based on the reliability of a portion of the scale, can be computed by using the Spearman-Brown formula, discussed earlier in this chapter. Recall that, according to this formula, reliability equals:

$$\frac{k\bar{r}}{1 + (k - 1)\bar{r}}$$

where k is the number of items in question and $\bar{r}$ is the average correlation of any one item with any other (i.e., the average inter-item correlation). If you had determined the reliability of a subset of items (e.g., by means of the split-half method) and knew how many items that reliability was based on (e.g., half the number in the whole scale), you could use the formula to compute $\bar{r}$. Then, you could plug that value of $\bar{r}$ and the number of items in the *whole* scale back into the formula. The result would be an estimate of the reliability of the *whole* scale, based on a reliability value computed on split halves of the scale. It simplifies matters if you perform a little algebra on the Spearman-Brown equation to put it into the following form:

$$\bar{r} = (r_{yy}) / [k - (k - 1)r_{yy}]$$

where r_{yy} is the reliability of the item set in question. For example, if you knew that the split-half reliability for two 9-item halves was equal to .90, you could compute $\bar{r}$ as follows:

$$\bar{r} = .9 / [9 - (8)(.9)]$$
$$= .5$$

You could then recompute the reliability for the whole 18-item scale by using $\bar{r} = .5$ and $k = 18$ in the Spearman-Brown formula. Thus, the reliability estimate for the full scale is:

$$\frac{18 \times .5}{1 + (17 \times .5)}$$

which equals 9/9.5 or .947. (Note that increasing the number of items has increased the reliability. A quick look at the Spearman-Brown formula should make it apparent that, all else being equal, a longer scale will always be more reliable than a shorter one.)

Temporal stability. Another two-score method of computing reliability involves the temporal stability of a measure, or how constant scores remain from one occasion to another. *Test-retest reliability* is the method typically used to assess this. Suppose that, instead of developing two sets of items to measure patients' desire for control when interacting with physicians, our hypothetical investigator developed only a single set. Those items could be given to one group of patients on two separate occasions, and the scores from the first occasion could be correlated with those from the later administration. The rationale underlying reliability determinations of this type is that if a measure truly reflects some meaningful construct, it should assess that construct comparably on separate occasions. In other words, the true score of the latent variable should exert comparable influence on observed scores on two (or more) occasions, while the error component should not remain constant across administrations of the scale. Consequently, the correlation of scores obtained across two administrations of a scale to the same individuals should represent the extent to which the latent variable determines observed scores. This is the equivalent to the definition of reliability as the proportion of variance attributable to the true score of the latent variable.

The problem with this reasoning is that what happens to the scores over time may or may not have to do with the error-proneness of the measurement procedure. Nunnally (1978) points out that characteristics of the items might cause them to yield temporally stable responses even when the construct of interest has changed. For example, if a purported anxiety measure was influenced by social desirability as well as anxiety, scores might remain constant despite variations in anxiety. The stability in scores, reflected in a high correlation across occasions of administration, would not be the result of invariance in the phenomenon of interest. Alternatively, the phenomenon may not change while scores on the measure do; that is, the scale could be unreliable. Or, changes in scores may be attributed to unreliability when, in fact, the phenomenon itself has changed and the measure has accurately tracked that change. The problem is that either a change or the absence of a change can be due to a variety of things besides the (un)reliability of the measurement procedure. Kelly and McGrath (1988) have identified four factors that are confounded when one examines two sets of scores on the same measure, separated in time. These are (a) real change in the construct of interest (e.g., a net increase in average level of anxiety among a sample of individuals), (b) systematic oscillations in the phenomenon (e.g., variations in anxiety, around some constant mean, as a function of time of day), (c) changes attributable to differences in subjects or measurement methods rather than the phenomenon of interest (e.g., fatigue effects that cause items to be misread), and (d) temporal instability due to the inherent unreliability of the measurement procedure. Only (d) is unreliability. These authors also note that, although methods such as the multitrait-multimethod matrix approach (discussed in the next chapter) can help, it is never possible to unconfound these factors fully.

This is not to say that demonstrating temporal stability is unimportant. In any number of research contexts, it may be critical to assume (or demonstrate) that measurements separated in time are highly correlated. However, the stability we seek in these situations is stability of *both* the *measure* and the *phenomenon*. Test-retest correlations only tell us about the measure when we are highly confident that the phenomenon has remained stable. Such confidence is not often warranted. Thus test-retest reliability, although important, may best be thought of as revealing something about the nature of a phenomenon *and* its measurement, not the latter alone. Referring to invariance in scores over time as *temporal stability* is preferable because it does not suggest, as does test-retest reliability, that measurement error is the source of any instability we observe.

GENERALIZABILITY THEORY

Thus far, our discussion of reliability has focused on partitioning observed variation into the portion that is attributable to the true score of the latent variable and the remaining portion, which is error. This section briefly introduces a more general framework for partitioning variance among error and nonerror sources.

Before we apply the idea of a finer partitioning of error variance to measurement, let us consider a more general research example in which multiple sources of variation are examined. Suppose that a researcher wanted to determine the effectiveness of a training program intended to increase professional productivity. Assume, furthermore, that the researcher administered the training program to a large sample of college professors and to a comparable sample of artists. The researcher also identified comparable groups of professors and artists who would not participate in the training program but who would take part in the same productivity assessment as the training program participants. Upon giving the study some thought, this researcher might have concluded that the observations of productivity would reflect the operation of three identifiable sources of systematic variation: (a) participant versus nonparticipant, (b) professor versus artist, and (c) the interaction of these effects. A reasonable analytic strategy in this situation would be to perform an analysis of variance (ANOVA) on the productivity scores, treating each of these sources of variation as a dimension in the analysis. The investigator could then determine to what extent each source of variation contributed to the total variation in professional productivity. In essence, this analytic strategy would partition the total variance among observed productivity scores into several sources: training participation, profession, the interaction of these, and error. Error would represent all sources of variation other than those specified by the preceding factors.

Now, consider a hypothetical situation in which a researcher is developing a scale of desire for autonomy. The measure will be used in a study of elderly people, some of whom may have visual problems. Consequently, the investigator plans to administer the desire-for-autonomy measure orally to those people who would have difficulty reading, and in written form to the remaining study participants.

If the researcher ignored mode of administration (written versus oral) as a source of variation in test scores, he or she would be regarding each score obtained as due to the true level of the respondent's desire for autonomy plus some degree of error. The researcher could proceed to calculate reliability as discussed earlier. Note, however, that merely computing alpha on the scale scores without regard for the mode of administration would not differentiate the potential systematic error due to administration method from any other source of error.

Alternatively, it is possible for the researcher to acknowledge administration mode as a source of variation among scores, using an analysis of variance approach. If the resulting analysis demonstrated that the difference between administration methods accounted for an inconsequential proportion of the total variation in scores, then the researcher could have greater confidence in the comparability of scores for individuals completing either the oral or written version. If, on the other hand, a significant amount of the total observed variation in scores were attributable to administration mode, then the researcher would know that any interpretation of scores should take this difference between modes into consideration.

Generalizability theory (Cronbach, Gleser, Nanda, & Rajaratnam, 1972) provides a framework for examining the extent to which one can assume equivalence of a measurement process across one or more dimensions. In the preceding example, the dimension in question was mode of administration. Each dimension of interest is a potential source of variation and is referred to as a *facet*. The example focused on mode of administration as the only potential source of variation (other than individuals) across which the investigator wished to generalize. Therefore, this example involves a single facet.

In the parlance of generalizability theory, observations obtainable across all levels of a facet (e.g., with both oral and written administration of the scale) constitute a *universe of admissible observations*. The mean of these observations is referred to as the *universe score* and is analogous to the true score of classical test theory (Allen & Yen, 1979). A study aimed at determining to what extent scores are comparable across different levels of a facet is called a generalizability study, or *G-study*. The hypothetical study of desire for autonomy is an example of a G-study by virtue of its addressing the effects of different "levels" of the mode-of-administration facet.

The purpose of the G-study is to help the investigator determine the extent to which the facet does or does not limit generalizability. If a facet (e.g., mode of administration) explains a significant amount of the variance in observed scores, findings *do not* generalize across levels (e.g., oral versus written administration) of that facet. The extent to which one can generalize across levels of the facet without misrepresenting the data is expressed as a *generalizability coefficient*. This is typically computed by forming a ratio from the appropriate mean squares resulting from the ANOVA performed as part of the G-study. Conceptually, the generalizability coefficient is the ratio of universe score variance to observed score variance and is analogous to the reliability coefficient (Allen & Yen, 1979). Note, however, that if a G-study yields a poor generalizability coefficient, the study s design points to a source of the problem—i.e., the facet examined. A reliability coefficient merely identifies the amount of error without attributing it to a specific source.

In some instances, choosing the appropriate ANOVA design, deciding which effects correspond to the facets of interest, and constructing the correct generalizability coefficient can be demanding. Just as with analysis of variance in general, multiple dimensions, nested, crossed, and mixed effects can complicate a G-study. (See Myers [1979] for a general discussion of ANOVA designs.) Keeping the design of a G-study simple is advisable. It is also prudent to consult a source that explains in detail how to build the appropriate ANOVA model for a given type of G-study. Crocker and Algina (1986) describe the appropriate designs for several different one- and two-facet generalizability studies. This source also provides a good general introduction to generalizability theory.

SUMMARY

Scales are reliable to the extent that they are comprised of reliable items that share a common latent variable. Coefficient alpha corresponds closely to the classical definition of reliability as the proportion of variance in a scale that is attributable to the true score of the latent variable. Various methods for computing reliability have different utility in particular situations. For example, if one does not have access to parallel versions of a scale, computing alternate forms reliability is impossible. A researcher who understands the advantages and disadvantages of alternative methods for computing reliability is in a better position to make informed judgments when designing a measurement study or evaluating a published report.

EXERCISES[2]

1. If a set of items has good internal consistency, what does that imply about the relationship of the items to their latent variable?

2. In this exercise,[3] assume that the following is a covariance matrix for a scale, Y, made up of three items X_1, X_2, and X_3:

$$\begin{bmatrix} 1.2 & .5 & .4 \\ .5 & 1.0 & .6 \\ .4 & .6 & 1.8 \end{bmatrix}$$

(a) What are the variances of X_1, X_2, and X_3?

(b) What is the variance of Y?

(c) What is coefficient alpha for scale Y?

3. Discuss the ways in which test-retest reliability confounds other factors with the actual scale properties.

4. How does the logic of alternate forms reliability follow from the assumptions of parallel tests?

NOTES

1. For weighted items, covariances are multiplied by products and variances by squares of their corresponding item weights. See Nunnally, 1978, pp. 154-156, for a more complete description.

2. Throughout the book, the solution for any exercise requiring a numeric answer will appear in a Note.

3. The answers are: (a) 1.2, 1.0, and 1.8 (which sum to 4.0); (b) 7.0 (the sum of all elements in the matrix); (c) $(3/2) * [1 - (4/7)] = 0.64$.

4

Validity

Whereas *reliability* concerns how much a variable influences a set of items, *validity* concerns whether *the* variable is the underlying cause of item covariation. To the extent that a scale is reliable, variation in scale scores can be attributed to the true score of some phenomenon that exerts a causal influence over all the items. However, determining that a scale is reliable does not guarantee that the latent variable shared by the items is, in fact, the variable of interest to the scale developer. The adequacy of a scale as a measure of a *specific variable* (e.g., perceived psychological stress) is an issue of validity.

Validity is inferred from the manner in which a scale was constructed, its ability to predict specific events, or its relationship to measures of other constructs. There are essentially three types of validity that correspond to these operations:

1. content validity
2. criterion-related validity
3. construct validity

Each type will be reviewed briefly. For a more extensive treatment of validity, including a discussion of methodological and statistical issues in criterion-related validity and alternative validity indices, see Chapter 10 in Ghiselli et al. (1981).

CONTENT VALIDITY

Content validity concerns item sampling adequacy—that is, the extent to which a specific set of items reflects a content domain. Content validity is easiest to evaluate when the domain (e.g., all the vocabulary words taught to sixth graders) is well defined. The issue is more subtle when measuring attributes, such as beliefs, attitudes, or dispositions, because it is difficult to determine exactly what the range of potential items is and when a sample of items is representative. In theory, a scale has content validity when its items are a randomly chosen subset of the universe of appropriate items. In the vocabulary test example used above, this is easily accomplished. All the words taught during the school year would be defined as the universe of items. Some subset could then be sampled. However, in the case of measuring beliefs, for example, we do not have a convenient listing of the relevant universe of items. Still, one's methods in developing a scale (e.g., having items reviewed by experts for relevance to the domain of interest, as suggested in Chapter 5) can help to maximize item appropriateness. For example, if a researcher needed to develop a measure contrasting expected outcomes and desired outcomes (e.g., expecting versus wanting a physician to involve the patient in decision making), it might be desirable to establish that all relevant outcomes were represented in the items. To do this, the researcher might have colleagues familiar with the context of the research review an initial list of items and suggest content areas that have been omitted but should be included. Items reflecting this content could then be added.

CRITERION-RELATED VALIDITY

In order to have criterion-related validity, as the term implies, an item or scale is required only to have an empirical association with some criterion or "gold standard." Whether or not the theoretical basis for that association is understood is irrelevant for criterion-related validity. If one could show, for example, that dowsing is empirically associated with locating underground water sources, then dowsing would have validity with respect to the criterion of successful well digging. Thus criterion-related validity per se is more a practical issue than a scientific one because it is not concerned with understanding a process but merely with predicting it. In fact, criterion-related validity is often referred to as *predictive validity.*

Criterion-related validity by any name does not necessarily imply a causal relationship among variables, even when the time ordering of the predictor and the criterion are unambiguous. Of course, prediction in the context of theory (e.g., prediction as a hypothesis) *may* be relevant to the causal relationships among variables and can serve a very useful scientific purpose.

Another point worth noting about criterion-related validity is that, logically, one is dealing with the same type of validity issue whether the criterion follows, precedes, or coincides with the measurement in question. Thus in addition to "predictive validity," *concurrent validity* (e.g., "predicting" driving skill from answers to oral questions asked during the driving test) or even *postdictive validity* (e.g., "predicting" birth weight from an infancy developmental status scale) may be used more or less synonymously with criterion-related validity. The most important aspect of criterion-related validity is not the time relationship between the measure in question and the criterion whose value one is attempting to infer but, rather, the strength of the empirical relationship between the two events. The term *criterion-related validity* has the advantage over the other terms of being temporally neutral and thus is preferable.

Criterion-related validity versus accuracy. Before leaving criterion-related validity, a few words are in order concerning its relationship to accuracy. As Ghiselli et al. (1981) point out, the correlation coefficient, which has been the traditional index of criterion-related validity, may not be very useful when *predictive accuracy* is the issue. A correlation coefficient, for example, does not reveal how many cases are correctly classified by a predictor (although tables that provide an estimate of the proportion of cases falling into various percentile categories, based on the size of the correlation between predictor and criterion, are described by Ghiselli et al., p. 311). It may be more appropriate in some situations to divide both a predictor and its criterion into discrete categories and to assess the "hit rate" for placing cases into the correct category of the criterion based on their predictor category. For example, one could classify each variable into "low" versus "high" categories, and conceptualize accuracy as the proportion of correct classifications (i.e., instances when the value of the predictor corresponds to the value of the criterion).

Also, it is important to remember that, even if the correlation between a predictor measure and a criterion is perfect, the *score* obtained on the predictor is *not an estimate* of the criterion. Correlation coefficients are insensitive to linear transformations of one or both variables. Transforming the predictor's units of measurement to that of the criterion may be necessary to obtain an accurate numerical prediction. This adjustment is equivalent to determining the appropriate intercept in addition to the slope of a regression line. A failure to recognize the need to transform a score could lead to erroneous conclusions. An error of this sort is perhaps most likely to occur if the predictor happens to be calibrated in units that fall into the same range as the criterion. Assume, for example, that someone devised the following "speeding ticket scale" to predict how many tickets drivers would receive over 5 years:

1. I exceed the speed limit when I drive.
   Frequently : Occasionally : Rarely : Never
2. On multi-lane roads, I drive in the passing lane.
   Frequently : Occasionally : Rarely : Never
3. I judge for myself what driving speed is appropriate.
   Frequently : Occasionally : Rarely : Never

Let us also make the implausible assumption that the scale correlates perfectly with the number of tickets received in a 5-year period. The scale is scored by giving each item a value of 3 when a respondent circles "frequently," 2 for "occasionally," 1 for "rarely," and 0 for "never." The item scores then are summed to get a scale score. The score's perfect criterion validity does not mean that a score of "9" translates into nine tickets over 5 years. Some empirically determined transformation (e.g., .33 ∗ SCORE) would yield the actual estimate. This particular transformation would predict three tickets for a driver scoring "9." If criterion-related validity were high, then a more accurate estimate could be computed. However, the similarity between the numerical values of the criterion and the predictor measure prior to an appropriate transformation would have nothing to do with the degree of validity.

CONSTRUCT VALIDITY

Construct validity (Cronbach & Meehl, 1955) is directly concerned with the theoretical relationship of a variable (e.g., a score on some scale) to other variables. It is the extent to which a measure "behaves" the way that the construct it purports to measure should behave with regard to established measures of other constructs. So, for example, if we view some variable, based on theory, as positively related to constructs A and B, negatively related to C and D, and unrelated to X and Y, then a scale that purports to measure that construct should bear a similar relationship to measures of those constructs. In other words, our measure should be positively correlated to measures of constructs A and B, negatively correlated with measures of C and D, and uncorrelated with measures of X and Y. A depiction of these hypothesized relationships might look like the following in Figure 4.1:

	A	B	C	D	X	Y
Var.	+	+	−	−	0	0

Figure 4.1. Hypothesized Relationships of Variables

The extent to which empirical correlations matched the predicted pattern provides some evidence of how well the measure "behaves" like the variable it is supposed to measure.

Differentiating construct from criterion-related validity. People often confuse construct and criterion-related validity because the same exact correlation can serve either purpose. The difference resides more in the investigator's intent than in the value obtained. For example, an epidemiologist might attempt to determine which of a variety of measures obtained in a survey study correlate with health status. The intent might be merely to identify risk factors without concern (at least initially) for the underlying causal mechanisms linking scores on measures to health status. Validity, in this case, is the degree to which the scales can predict health status. Alternatively, the concern could be more theoretical and explanatory. The investigator, like the epidemiologist described in this book's opening chapter, might endorse a theoretical model that views stress as a cause of health status, and the issue might be how well a newly developed scale measures stress. This might be assessed by evaluating the "behavior" of the scale relative to how theory suggests stress should operate. If the theory suggested that stress and health status should be correlated, then the same empirical relationship used as evidence of predictive validity in the preceding example might be used as evidence of construct validity.

So-called *known-groups validation* is another example of a procedure that can be classified either as construct or criterion-related validity, depending on the investigator's intent. Known-groups validation typically involves demonstrating that some scale can differentiate members of one group from another, based on their scale scores. The purpose may be either theory related (as when a measure of attitudes toward a certain group is validated by correctly differentiating those who do or do not affiliate with members of that group) or purely predictive (as when one uses a series of seemingly unrelated items to predict job turnover). In the former case, the procedure should be considered a type of construct validity and in the latter, criterion-related validity.

How strong should correlations be in order to demonstrate construct validity? There is no cutoff that defines construct validity. It is important to recognize that two measures may share more than construct similarity. Specifically, similarities in the way that constructs are measured may account for some covariation in scores independent of construct similarity. For example, two variables scored on a multipoint scoring system (scores from 1 to 100) will have a higher correlation with each other than with a binary variable, all else being equal. This is an artifact caused by the structure of the measurement methods. Likewise, because of procedural similarities, data of one type gathered by interviews may correlate to a degree with other data gathered in the same way; that is, some of the covariation between two variables may be due to measurement similarity rather than construct similarity. This fact provides some basis for answering the question concerning the magnitude of correlations necessary to conclude construct validity. The variables, at a minimum, should demonstrate covariation above and beyond what can be attributed to shared method variance.

Multitrait-multimethod matrix. Campbell and Fiske (1959) devised a procedure called the multitrait-multimethod matrix that is extremely useful for examining construct validity. The procedure involves measuring more than one construct by means of more than one method so that one obtains a "fully crossed" method-by-measure matrix. For example, suppose that a study is designed in which anxiety and depression and shoe size are each measured at two times using two different measurement procedures each time. (Note that two different samples of individuals could have been measured at the same time. What effect would this have on the logic of the approach?) Each construct could be assessed by two methods, a visual analog scale (a line upon which respondents make a mark to indicate the amount of the attribute they possess, be it anxiety, depression, or bigness of foot) and a rating assigned by an interviewer following a 15-minute interaction with each subject. One could then construct a matrix of correlations obtained between measurements as follows in Table 4.1:

Table 4.1
Multitrait-Multimethod Matrix

		Time 1					
		A_v	A_i	D_v	D_i	S_v	S_i
	A_v	*	+	#		#	
	A_i	+	*		#		#
Time 2	D_v	#		*	+	#	
	D_i		#	+	*		#
	S_v	#		#		*	+
	S_i		#		#	+	*

* = same trait and method (reliability)
+ = same trait, different method
# = same method, different trait
NOTE: A, D, and S refer to the constructs anxiety, depression, and shoe size, respectively. Subscripts v and i refer to visual analog and interview methods, respectively.

Another possible distinction, not in the table, is between *related* versus *unrelated* traits.

Because the entries that reflect the same trait (construct) and the same method should share both method and construct variance, one would expect these correlations to be highest. It is hoped that correlations corresponding to the same trait but different methods would be the next highest. If so, this would suggest that construct covariation is higher than method covariation; in other words, our measures were more influenced by *what* was measured than by *how* it was measured. In contrast, there is no reason why any covariation should exist between shoe size and either of the other two constructs when they are measured by different procedures. Thus these correlations should not be significantly different from zero. For nonidentical but theoretically related constructs, such as depression and anxiety, one would expect some construct covariation. This is potentially a highly informative set of correlations for establishing construct validity. If, for example, our depression measures were both well established but our anxiety measures were currently being developed, we could assess the amount of covariation attributable to concept similarity under conditions of similar and different measurement procedures. Theory asserts that anxiety and depression should be substantially correlated even when measured by different methods. If this proved to be the case, it would serve as evidence of the construct validity of our new anxiety measures. More specifically, these correlations would be indicative of *convergent validity,* evidence of similarity between measures of theoretically related constructs. Ideally, the correlations between anxiety and depression would be less than those between two depression or two anxiety measures, but substantially greater than between either of the depression scores and shoe size. Equally important is evidence that the anxiety measures did not correlate significantly with measures of shoe size, irrespective of similarity or dissimilarity of measurement technique. This is evidence of *discriminant* (sometimes called divergent) validity, the absence of correlation between measures of unrelated constructs. Shoe size and anxiety correlating significantly when measured the same way would suggest that method per se accounted for a substantial amount of the variation (and covariation) associated with similar measures of the dissimilar constructs.

Mitchell (1979) observed that the methods involved in collecting data for a multitrait-multimethod matrix constitute a two-facet G-study (see Chapter 3), with traits and methods being the facets. The multitrait-multimethod matrix allows us to partition covariation into "method" and "trait" (or "construct") sources. We can then make more precise statements about construct validity because it allows us to differentiate covariation that truly reflects similarity of construct (and thus is relevant to construct validity) from covariation that is an artifact of applying similar measurement procedures (and thus does not relate to construct validity). Such a differentiation is not possible when one simply examines a single correlation between two measures.

EXERCISES

1. Give an example of how the same correlation between a scale and a behavior might be indicative of either construct validity or criterion-related validity. Explain how both (a) the motives behind computing the correlation and (b) the interpretation of that correlation would differ, depending on the type of validity the investigator was trying to assess.

2. Assume that an investigator has paper-and-pencil measures of two constructs: self-esteem and social conformity. The investigator also has interview-based scores on the same two constructs. How could these data be used in a multitrait-multimethod matrix to demonstrate that the method of data collection had an undesirably strong effect on the results obtained?

5

Guidelines in Scale Development

Thus far, our discussion has been fairly theoretical. We now look at how this theoretical knowledge can be applied. This chapter provides a set of specific guidelines that investigators can use in developing measurement scales.

STEP 1:
DETERMINE CLEARLY WHAT IT IS
YOU WANT TO MEASURE

This is deceptively obvious, and many researchers *think* they have a clear idea of what they wish to measure, only to find that their ideas are more vague than they thought. Frequently, this realization occurs after considerable effort has been invested in generating items and collecting data—a time when changes are far more costly than if discovered at the outset of the process. Should the scale be based in theory, or should you strike out in new intellectual directions? How specific should the measure be? Should some aspect of the phenomenon be emphasized more than others?

Theory as an aid to clarity. As noted in Chapter 1, thinking clearly about the content of a scale requires thinking clearly about the construct being measured. Although there are many technical aspects involved in developing and validating a scale, one should not overlook the importance of being well grounded in the substantive theories related to the phenomenon to be measured. The types of scales that are the focus of this book are intended to measure elusive phenomena that cannot be observed directly. Because there is no tangible criterion against which one can compare this type of scale's performance, it is important to have some clear ideas to serve as a guide. The boundaries of the phenomenon must be recognized so that the content of the scale does not inadvertently drift into unintended domains.

Theory is a great aid to clarity. Relevant social science theories should *always* be considered before developing a scale of the type discussed in

51

this volume. If it turns out that extant theory offers no guide to the scale developers, then they may decide that a new intellectual direction is necessary. However, this decision should be an informed one, reached only after reviewing appropriate theory related to the measurement problem at hand. Even if there is no available theory to guide the investigators, they must lay out their own conceptual formulations prior to trying to operationalize them. In essence, they must specify at least a tentative theoretical model that will serve as a guide to scale development. This may be as simple as a well-formulated definition of the phenomenon they seek to measure. Better still would be to include a description of how the new construct relates to existing phenomena and their operationalizations.

Specificity as an aid to clarity. The level of specificity or generality at which a construct is measured also may be very important. There is general agreement in the social sciences that variables will relate most strongly to one another when they match with respect to level of specificity (see Ajzen & Fishbein, 1980, for a discussion). Sometimes a scale is intended to relate to very specific behaviors or constructs while at other times a more general and global measure is sought.

As an illustration of measures that differ in specificity, consider the locus of control (LOC) construct. Locus of control is a widely used concept that concerns individuals' perceptions about who or what influences important outcomes in their lives. The construct can be applied broadly, as a means of explaining patterns of global behavior spanning many situations, or narrowly, to predict how an individual will respond in a very specific context. The sources of influence also can be described either broadly or specifically. Rotter's (1966) Internal-External (I-E) scale, for example, is concerned at a fairly general level with these perceptions. A single dimension ranging from personal control to control by outside factors underlies the scale, and the outcomes on which the items focus are general, such as personal success. The external sources of control also are described in general terms. The following external statement is from Rotter's I-E scale: "The world is run by the few people in power, and there is not much the little guy can do about it." Levenson (1973) developed a multidimensional LOC scale that allows for three loci of control: oneself, powerful other people, and chance or fate. This permits an investigator to look at external sources of control a bit more specifically by characterizing them as either powerful others or fate. The outcomes on which she focused, however, remained general. An example of an item from Levenson's Powerful Others subscale is, "I feel like what happens in my life is determined by powerful others." Wallston, et al. (1978) developed the Multidimensional Health Locus of Control (MHLC) scales using Levenson's three loci of control, with outcomes specific to health, such as avoiding illness or getting sick. A sample item from the Powerful Others scale of the MHLC is, "Having regular contact with my physician is the best way for me to avoid illness." More recently, K. Wallston (personal communication) has developed an even more outcome-specific health locus of control measure that consists of a series of "template" items. This measure allows the researcher to specify any health problem of interest by substituting the name of the illness or disorder for the phrase, "my condition," in each of the template items. A sample item from the Powerful Others scale of MHLC Form C, as it might be used in a study of diabetes, is, "If I see my doctor regularly, I am less likely to have problems with my diabetes."

Each of these progressively more specific LOC scales is useful. Which is most useful depends largely upon what level of outcome or locus generality relates to the scientific question being asked. For example, if a locus of control scale is intended to predict a general class of behavior or will be compared to other variables assessing constructs at a general level, then Rotter's scale may be the best choice because it, too, is general. On the other hand, if a researcher is interested in predicting specifically how beliefs about the influence of other people affects certain health behaviors, then the new Wallston scale may be more appropriate because the level of specificity matches that research question. During its development, each of these scales had a clear frame of reference that determined what level of specificity was appropriate, given the intended function of the scale. The point is that scale developers should make this determination as an active decision and not merely generate a set of items and then see what they look like after the fact.

The locus of control example illustrated specificity with respect to outcomes (e.g., how the world is run versus problems with diabetes) and the loci of control (i.e, external generally versus fate and powerful others separately). However, scale specificity can vary along a number of dimensions, including content domains (e.g., anxiety versus psychological adjustment more broadly), setting (e.g., questionnaires designed specifically for relevance to particular work environments), or population (e.g., children versus adults or military personnel versus college students).

Being clear about what to include in a measure. Scale developers should ask themselves if the construct they wish to measure is distinct from other constructs. As noted earlier, scales can be developed to be relatively broad or narrow with respect to the situations to which they apply. This is also the case with respect to the constructs they cover. Measuring general anxiety is perfectly legitimate. Such a measure might measure both test anxiety and social anxiety. This is fine if it matches the goals of the scale developer or user. However, if one is interested in only one specific type of anxiety, then the scale should exclude all others. Items that might "cross over" into a related construct (e.g., tapping social anxiety when the topic of interest is test anxiety) can be problematic.

Sometimes, apparently similar items may tap quite different constructs. In such cases, although the purpose of the scale may be to measure one phenomenon, it may also be sensitive to other phenomena. For example, certain depression measures, such as the Center for Epidemiological Studies Depression (CES-D) scale (Radloff, 1977), have some items that tap somatic aspects of depression (e.g., concerning the respondent's ability to "get going"). In the context of some health conditions such as arthritis, these items might mistake aspects of the illness for symptoms of depression (see Blalock, DeVellis, Brown, & Wallston, 1989, for a discussion of this specific point). A researcher developing a new depression scale might choose to avoid somatic items if the scale were to be used with certain populations (e.g., chronically ill) or with other measures of somatic constructs (such as hypochondriasis). Used for other purposes, of course, it might be very important to include somatic items, as when the line of investigation specifically concerns somatic aspects of negative affect.

STEP 2:
GENERATE AN ITEM POOL

Once the purpose of a scale has been clearly articulated, the developer is ready to begin constructing the instrument in earnest. The first step is to generate a large pool of items that are candidates for eventual inclusion in the scale.

Choose items that reflect the scale's purpose. Obviously, these items should be selected or created with the specific measurement goal in mind. The description of exactly what the scale is intended to do should guide this process. Recall that all items making up a homogenous scale should reflect the latent variable underlying them. Each item can be thought of as a "test," in its own right, of the strength of the latent variable. Therefore, the content of each item should primarily reflect the construct of interest. Multiple items will constitute a more reliable test than individual items, but each must still be sensitive to the true score of the latent variable. Theoretically, a good set of items is chosen randomly from the universe of items relating to the construct of interest. The universe of items is assumed to be infinitely large, which pretty much precludes any hope of actually identifying it and extracting items randomly. However, this ideal should be kept in mind. If you are writing items anew, as is so often the case, you should think creatively about the construct you seek to measure. What other ways can an item be worded so as to get at the construct? Although the items should not venture beyond the bounds of the defining construct, they should exhaust the possibilities for types of items within those bounds. The properties of a scale are determined by the items that make it up. If they are a poor reflection of the concept you have worked long and hard to articulate, then the scale will not accurately capture the essence of the construct.

It is also important that the "thing" that items have in common is truly a construct and not merely a category. Recall, once again, that our models for scale development regard items as overt manifestations of a common latent variable that is their cause. Scores on items related to a common construct are determined by the true score of that construct. However, as noted in Chapter 1, just because items relate to a common category does not guarantee that they have the same underlying latent variable. Such terms as attitudes, barriers to compliance, or life events often define categories of constructs rather than the constructs themselves. A pool of items that will eventually be the basis of a unidimensional scale should not merely share a focus on attitudes, for example. but on *specific* attitudes, such as attitudes toward punishing drug abusers. One can presumably envision a characteristic of the person, a latent variable, if you will, that would "cause" responses to items dealing with punishing drug abusers. It is quite a challenge to imagine a characteristic that accounts for attitudes in general. The same is true for the other examples cited. Barriers to compliance are typically of many types. Each type (e.g., fear of discovering symptoms, concern over treatment costs, anticipation of pain, distance of treatment facilities, perceptions of invulnerability) may represent a latent variable. There may even be nontrivial correlations among some of the latent variables. However, each of these barriers is a separate construct. Thus the term *barriers* describes a category of constructs rather than an individual construct related to a single latent variable. Items measuring different constructs that fall within the same category (e.g., perceptions of invulnerability and concerns over treatment costs) should not be expected to covary the way items do when they are manifestations of a common latent variable.

Redundancy. At this stage of the scale development process, it is better to be overinclusive, all other things being equal. Redundancy is *not* a bad thing when developing a scale. In fact, the theoretical models that guide our scale development efforts are based on redundancy. In discussing the Spearman-Brown Prophecy formula in Chapter 3, I pointed out that reliability varies as a function of the number of items, all else being equal. We are attempting to capture the phenomenon of interest by developing a set of items that reveal the phenomenon in different ways. By using multiple and seemingly redundant items, the content that is common to the items will summate across items while their irrelevant idiosyncracies will cancel out. Without redundancy, this would be impossible. Useful redundancy pertains to the construct, not incidental aspects of the items. Changing nothing more than an "a" to "the" in an item will certainly give you redundancy with respect to the important content of the item but it will also be redundant with respect to many things that you want to vary, such as the basic grammatical structure and choice of words. On the other hand, two items, such as "I will do almost anything to ensure my child's success" and "No sacrifice is too great if it helps my child achieve success," may be usefully redundant because they express a similar idea in somewhat different ways.

You can tolerate considerably more redundancy in your item pool than in the final scale, even though some redundancy is desirable even in the latter. For example, if an item such as "In my opinion, pet lovers are kind" has been written, there may be little advantage in including an additional item that states, "In my estimation, pet lovers are kind." Although these items clearly tap similar sentiments regarding pet ownership, they also share a common grammatical structure and use nearly identical vocabularies. However, an item such as "I think that people who like pets are good people" might do a good job of being redundant with respect to the substantive content of the first item without trivial redundancy. However, at this very early stage of scale development, even the extreme redundancy between the first two items in this example might be acceptable, as long as only one appears on the final scale. Considering two items, even when they are as similar as these, might provide the scale developer with an opportunity to compare them and express a preference (e.g., "opinion" may seem less pretentious than "estimation"). This opportunity would be lost if only one of the two items were considered.

Number of items. It is impossible to specify the number of items that should be included in an initial pool. Suffice it to say that you want considerably more than you plan to include in the final scale. Recall that internal consistency reliability is a function of how strongly the items correlate with one another (and hence with the latent variable), and how many items you have in the scale. As the nature of the correlations among items is usually not known at this stage of scale development, having lots of items is a form of insurance against poor internal consistency. The more items you have in your pool, the fussier you can be about choosing ones that will do the job you intend. It would not be unusual to begin with a pool of items that is three or four times as large as the final scale. Thus a 10-item scale might evolve from a 40-item pool. If items are particularly difficult to generate for a given content area or if empirical data indicate that numerous items are not needed to attain good internal consistency, then the initial pool may be as small as 50% larger than the final scale.

In general, the larger the item pool, the better. However, it is certainly possible to develop a pool too large to administer on a single occasion to any one group of subjects. If the pool is exceptionally large, the researcher can eliminate some items based on a priori criteria, such as lack of clarity, questionable relevance, or undesirable similarity to other items.

Characteristics of good and bad items. Listing all the things that make an item good or bad is an impossible task. The content domain, obviously, has a significant bearing on item quality. However, there are some characteristics that reliably separate better items from worse ones. Most of these relate to clarity. As pointed out in Chapter 1, a good item should be unambiguous. Questions that leave the respondent in a quandary should be eliminated.

Scale developers should avoid *exceptionally lengthy items,* as length usually increases complexity and diminishes clarity. However, it is not desirable to sacrifice the meaning of an item in the interest of brevity. If a modifying clause is essential to convey the intent of an item, then include it. However, avoid unnecessary wordiness. In general, an item such as "I often have difficulty making a point" will be better than an unnecessarily longer one, such as "It is fair to say that one of the things I seem to have a problem with much of the time is getting my point across to other people."

Another related consideration in choosing or developing items is the *reading difficulty level* at which the items are written. There are a variety of methods (e.g., Dale & Chall, 1948; Fry, 1977) for assigning grade levels to passages of prose, including scale items. These typically equate longer words and sentences with higher reading levels. Reading most local newspapers presumably requires a sixth-grade reading level.

Fry (1977) delineates several steps to quantifying reading level. The first is to select a sample of text that begins with the first word of a sentence and contains exactly 100 words. (For scales having only a few items, you may have to select a convenient fraction of 100 and base subsequent steps on this proportion.) Next, count the number of complete sentences and individual syllables in the text sample. These values are used as entry points for a graph that provides grade equivalents for different combinations of sentence and syllable counts from the 100-word sample. The graph indicates that the average number of words and syllables per sentence for a fifth-grade reading level are 14 and 18, respectively. An average sentence at the sixth-grade level has 15 or 16 words and a total of 20 syllables; a seventh-grade-level sentence has about 18 words and 24 syllables. Shorter sentences with a higher proportion of longer words or longer sentences with fewer long words can yield an equivalent grade level. For example, a sentence of 9 words and 13 syllables (i.e., as many as 44% polysyllabic words) or one with 19 words and 22 syllables (i.e., no more than about 14% polysyllabic words) are both classified as sixth-grade reading level. Aiming for a reading level between the fifth and seventh grades is probably an appropriate target for most instruments that will be used with the general population. The items of the Multidimensional Health Locus of Control (MHLC) scales, for example, were written at a fifth- to seventh-grade reading level. A typical item at this reading level is: "Most things that affect my health happen to me by accident" (Wallston et al., 1978). Its 9 words and 15 syllables place it at the sixth-grade level.

Fry (1977) notes that semantic and syntactic factors should be considered in assessing reading difficulty. Because short words tend to be more common and short sentences tend to be syntactically simpler, his procedure is an acceptable alternative to more complex difficulty-assessment methods. However, as with other criteria for writing or choosing good items, one must use common sense in applying reading level methods. Some brief phrases containing only short words are not elementary. "Eschew casque scorn," for example, is more likely to confuse someone with a grade-school education than "Wear your helmet" will, despite the fact that both have three words and four syllables. Another source of potential confusion that should be avoided is *multiple negatives*. "I am not in favor of corporations stopping funding for anti-nuclear groups" is much more confusing than "I favor continued private support of groups advocating a nuclear ban." (It is also instructive to observe that these two statements might convey different positions on the issue. For example, the latter might imply a preference for private over public support of the groups in question.)

So-called *double barreled* items should also be avoided. These are items that convey two or more ideas so that an endorsement of the item might refer to either or both ideas. "I support civil rights because discrimination is a crime against God" is an example of a double-barreled item. If a person supports civil rights for reasons other than its affront to a deity (e.g., because it is a crime against humanity), how should he or she answer? A negative answer might incorrectly convey a lack of support for civil rights, and a positive answer might incorrectly ascribe a motive to the respondent's support.

Another problem that scale developers should avoid is *ambiguous pronoun references.* "Murderers and rapists should not seek pardons from politicians because they are the scum of the earth" might express the sentiments of some people irrespective of pronoun reference. (However, a scale developer usually intends to be more clear about what an item means.) This sentence should be twice cursed. In addition to the ambiguous pronoun reference, it is double-barreled. *Misplaced modifiers* create ambiguities similar to ambiguous pronoun references: "Our representatives should work diligently to legalize prostitution in the House of Representatives" is an example of such modifiers. Using *adjective forms instead of noun forms* can also create unintended confusion. Consider the differences in meaning between "All vagrants should be given a schizophrenic assessment" and "All vagrants should be given a schizophrenia assessment."

Positively and negatively worded items. Many scale developers choose to write *negatively worded items,* items that represent low levels or even the absence of the construct of interest, as well as the more common *positively worded items* that represent its presence. The goal is to arrive at a set of items, some of which indicate a high level of the latent variable when endorsed and others that indicate a high level when not endorsed. The Rosenberg (1965) Self-Esteem (RSE) scale, for example, includes items indicative of high esteem (e.g., "I feel that I have a number of good qualities") and of low esteem (e.g., "I certainly feel useless at times"). The intent of wording items both positively and negatively within the same scale is usually to avoid an *acquiescence, affirmation, or agreement bias.* These interchangeable terms refer to a respondent's tendency to agree with items irrespective of their content. If, for example, a scale consists of items that express a high degree of self-esteem, then an acquiescence bias would result in a pattern of responses appearing to indicate very high esteem. If the scale is made up of equal numbers of positively and negatively worded items, on the other hand, then an acquiescence bias and an extreme degree of self-esteem could be differentiated from one another by the pattern of responses. An "agreer" would endorse items indicating both high and low self-esteem, whereas a person who truly had high esteem would strongly endorse high-esteem items and negatively endorse low-esteem items.

Unfortunately, there may be a price to pay for including positively and negatively worded items. Reversals in item polarity may be confusing to respondents, especially when completing a long questionnaire. In such a case, the respondents may become confused about the difference between expressing their strength of agreement with a statement, regardless of its polarity, versus expressing the strength of the attribute being measured (esteem, for example). Perhaps the best course is for the scale developer to be aware of both the acquiescence and confusion problems and to write questions and instructions as clearly as possible.

Conclusion. An item pool should be a rich source from which a scale can emerge. It should contain a large number of items that are relevant to the content of interest. Redundancy with respect to content is an asset, not a liability. It is the foundation of internal consistency reliability which, in turn, is the foundation of validity. Items should not involve a "package deal" that makes it impossible for respondents to endorse one part of the item without endorsing another part that may not be consistent with the first. Whether or not positively and negatively worded items are both included in the pool, their wording should follow established rules of grammar. This will help to avoid some of the sources of ambiguity discussed above.

STEP 3:
DETERMINE THE FORMAT
FOR MEASUREMENT

Numerous formats for questions exist. The researcher should consider early on what the format will be. This step should occur simultaneously with the generation of items so that the two are compatible. For example, generating a long list of declarative statements may be a waste of time if the response format eventually chosen is a checklist comprised of single-word items. Furthermore, the theoretical models presented earlier are more consistent with some response formats than with others. In general, scales made up of items that are scorable on some continuum and that are summed to form a scale score are most compatible with the theoretical orientation presented in this volume. In this section, however, I will discuss common formats that depart from the pattern implied by the theoretical models discussed in Chapter 2, as well as ones that adhere to that pattern.

Thurstone scaling. There are a number of general strategies for constructing scales that influence the format of items and response options. One method is *Thurstone scaling.* An analogy may help to clarify how Thurstone scaling works. A tuning fork is designed to vibrate at a specific frequency. If you strike it, it will vibrate at that frequency and produce a specific tone. Conversely, if you place the fork near a tone source that produces the same frequency as the tuning fork, the fork will begin to vibrate. In a sense, then, a tuning fork is a "frequency detector," vibrating in the presence of sound waves of its resonant frequency and remaining motionless in the presence of all other frequencies. Imagine a series of tuning forks aligned in an array such that as one moves from left to right along the array, the tuning forks correspond to progressively higher frequency sounds. Within the range of the tuning forks' frequency, this array can be used to identify the frequency of a tone. In other words, you could identify the tone's frequency by seeing which fork vibrated when the tone was played. A Thurstone scale is intended to work in the same way. The scale developer attempts to generate items that are differentially responsive to specific levels of the attribute in question. When the "pitch" of a particular item matches the level of the attribute a respondent possesses, the item will signal this correspondence. Often, the "signal" consists of an affirmative response for items that are "tuned" to the appropriate level of the attribute and a negative response for all other items. The "tuning" (i.e., determination of what level of the construct each item responds to) is typically determined by having judges place a large pool of items into piles corresponding to equally spaced intervals of construct magnitude or strength.

This is quite an elegant idea. Items could be developed that correspond to different intensities of the attribute, spaced to represent equal intervals, and could be formatted with agree-disagree response options, for example. The investigator could give these items to respondents and then inspect their responses to see which items triggered agreement. Because the items would have been precalibrated with respect to their sensitivity to specific levels of the phenomenon, the agreements would pinpoint how much of the attribute the respondent possessed. The selection of items to represent equal intervals across items would result in highly desirable measurement properties because scores would be amenable to mathematical procedures based on interval scaling.

Part of a hypothetical Thurstone scale for measuring parents' aspirations for their children's educational and career attainments might look like the following:

1. Achieving success is the only way for my
   child to repay my efforts as a parent   Agree _____ Disagree _____

2. Going to a good college and getting a
   good job are important but not essential
   to my child's happiness   Agree _____ Disagree _____

3. Happiness has nothing to do with achieving
   educational or material goals   Agree _____ Disagree _____

4. The customarily valued trappings of success
   are a hindrance to true happiness   Agree _____ Disagree _____

As Nunnally (1978) points out, developing a true Thurstone scale is considerably harder than describing one. Finding items that consistently "resonate" to specific levels of the phenomenon is quite difficult. The practical problems associated with the method often outweigh its advantages unless the researcher has a compelling reason for wanting the type of calibration that it provides. Although Thurstone scaling is an interesting and sometimes suitable approach, it will not be referred to herein henceforth.

Guttman scaling. A *Guttman scale* is a series of items tapping progressively higher levels of an attribute. Thus a respondent should endorse a block of adjacent items until, at a critical point, the amount of the attribute that the items tap exceeds that possessed by the subject. None of the remaining items should be endorsed. Some purely descriptive data conform to a Guttman scale. For example, a series of interview questions might ask, "Do you smoke?" "Do you smoke more than 10 cigarettes a day?" "Do you smoke more than a pack a day?" and so on. As with this example, endorsing any specific item on a Guttman scale implies affirmation of all preceding items. A respondent's level of the attribute is indicated by the highest item yielding an affirmative response. Note that, whereas both Thurstone and Guttman scales are made up of graded items, the focus is on a single affirmative response in the former case but the point of transition from affirmative to negative responses is the focus of the latter. A Guttman version of the preceding parental aspiration scale might look like this:

1. Achieving success is the only way for my child to repay my efforts as a parent   Agree _____ Disagree _____

2. Going to a good college and getting a good job are very important to my child's happiness   Agree _____ Disagree _____

3. Happiness is more likely if a person has attained his or her educational and material goals   Agree _____ Disagree _____

4. The customarily valued trappings of success are not a hindrance to true happiness   Agree _____ Disagree _____

Guttman scales can work quite well for objective information or in situations where it is a logical necessity that responding positively to one level of a hierarchy implies satisfying the criteria of all lower levels of that hierarchy. Things get murkier when the phenomenon of interest is not concrete. In the case of our hypothetical parental aspiration scale, for example, the ordering may not be uniform across individuals. Whereas 20 cigarettes a day always implies more smoking than 10, responses to items 3 and 4 in the parental aspiration scale example may not always conform to the ordering pattern of a Guttman scale. For example, a person might agree with item 3 but disagree with item 4. Ordinarily, agreement with item 3 would imply agreement with 4, but if a respondent viewed success as a complex factor that acted simultaneously as a help and a hindrance to happiness, then an atypical pattern of responses could result.

Like Thurstone scales, Guttman scales undoubtedly have their place, but their applicability seems rather limited. With both approaches, the disadvantages and difficulties will often outweigh the advantages. It is also important to reiterate that the measurement theories discussed thus far do not always apply to these types of scales. Certainly, the assumption of equally strong causal relationships between the latent variable and each of the items would not apply to Thurstone or Guttman scale items. Nunnally (1978) describes briefly some of the conceptual models underlying these scales.

Scales with equally weighted items. The measurement models discussed earlier fit best with scales consisting of items that are more or less

equivalent "detectors" of the phenomenon of interest—that is, they are
more or less parallel (but not necessarily parallel in the strict sense of the
Parallel Tests model). They are imperfect indicators of a common phenomenon that can be combined by simple summation into an acceptably
reliable scale.

One attractive feature of scales of this type is that the individual items
can have a variety of response option formats. This allows the scale
developer a good deal of latitude in constructing a measure optimally
suited for a particular purpose. Some general issues related to response
formatting will be examined below, as will the merits and liabilities of
some representative response formats.

How many response categories? Most scale items consist of two parts:
a stem and a series of response options. For example, the stem of each
item may be a different declarative statement expressing an opinion, and
the response options accompanying each stem might be a series of
descriptors indicating the strength of agreement with the statement. For
now, let us focus on the response options—specifically, the number of
choices that should be available to the respondent. Some item response
formats allow the subject an infinite or very large number of options,
whereas others limit the possible responses. Imagine, for example, a
response scale for measuring anger that resembles a thermometer, calibrated from "no anger at all" at the base of the thermometer to "complete,
uncontrollable rage" at its top. A respondent could be presented with a
series of situation descriptions, each accompanied by a copy of the
thermometer scale, and asked to indicate, by shading in some portion of
the thermometer, how much anger the situation provoked. This method
allows for virtually continuous measurement of anger. An alternative
method might ask the respondent to indicate, using a number from 1 to
100, how much anger each situation provoked. This provides for numerous discrete responses. Alternatively, the format could restrict the response options to a few choices, such as "none," "a little," "a moderate
amount," and "a lot," or to a simple binary selection between "angry" and
"not angry."

What are the relative advantages of these alternatives? A desirable
quality of a measurement scale is variability. A measure cannot covary if
it does not vary. If a scale fails to discriminate differences in the underlying attribute, its correlations with other measures will be restricted and
its utility will be limited. One way to increase opportunities for variability
is to have lots of scale items. Another is to have numerous response
options within items. If circumstances restrict an investigator to two

questions regarding anger, for example, it might be best to allow respondents more latitude in describing their level of anger. Assume that the research concerns the enforcement of nonsmoking policies in a work setting. Let us further assume that the investigators want to determine the relationship between policy and anger. If they were limited to only two questions (e.g., "How much anger do you feel when you are restricted from smoking?" and "How much anger do you feel when you are exposed to others smoking in the work place?"), they might get more useful information from a response format that allowed subjects many gradations of response than from a binary response format. For example, a 0-to-100 scale might reveal wide differences in reactions to these situations and yield good variability for the two-item scale. On the other hand, if the research team were allowed to include 50 questions about smoking and anger, simple "angry" versus "not angry" indications might yield sufficient variability when the items are added to obtain a scale score. In fact, being faced with more response options on each of 50 questions might fatigue or bore the respondents, lowering the reliability of their responses.

Another issue related to the number of response options is the *respondents' ability to discriminate meaningfully*. How fine a distinction can the typical subject make? This obviously depends on what is being measured. Few things can truly be evaluated into, say, 50 discrete categories. Presented with this many options, many respondents may use only those corresponding to multiples of 5 or 10, effectively reducing the number of options to as few as five. Differences between a response of 35 and 37 may not reflect actual difference in the phenomenon being measured. Little is gained with this sort of false precision. Although the scale's variance might increase, it may be the random (i.e., error) portion rather than the systematic portion attributable to the underlying phenomenon that is increasing. This, of course, offers no benefit.

Sometimes the respondent's ability to discriminate meaningfully between response options will depend on the *specific wording or physical placement* of those options. Asking a respondent to discriminate among vague quantity descriptors, such as "several," "few," and "many," may create problems. Sometimes the ambiguity can be reduced by the arrangement of the response options on the page. Respondents often seem to understand what is desired when they are presented with an obvious continuum. Thus an ordering such as:

Many	Some	Few	Very few	None

may imply that "some" is more than "few" because of the ordering of these items. However, if it is possible to find a nonambiguous adjective that precludes the respondents' making assumptions based on location along a continuum, so much the better. At times, it may be preferable to have fewer response options than to have ones that are ambiguous. So, for example, it may be better in the above example to eliminate either "some" or "few" and have four options rather than five. The worst circumstance is to combine ambiguous words with ambiguous page locations. Consider the following example:

Very helpful   Not very helpful
Somewhat helpful   Not at all helpful

Terms such as "somewhat" and "not very" are difficult to differentiate under the best of circumstances. However, arranging these response options as they appear above makes matters even worse. If a respondent reads down the first column and then down the second, "somewhat" appears to represent a higher value than "not very." But, if a respondent reads across the first row and then across the second, the implicit ordering of these two descriptors along the continuum is reversed. Due to ambiguity in both language and spatial arrangement, individuals may assign different meanings to the two options representing moderate values, and reliability would suffer as a consequence.

Still another issue is the *investigator's ability and willingness to record a large number of values* for each item. If the thermometer method described earlier is used to quantify anger responses, is the researcher actually going to attempt a precise scoring of each response? How much precision is appropriate? Can the shaded area be measured to within a quarter of an inch? A centimeter? A millimeter? If only some crude datum, say lower, middle, or upper third, is extracted from the scale, what was the point in requesting such a precise response?

There is at least one more issue related to the number of responses. Assuming that a few discrete responses are allowed for each item, *should the number be odd or even?* Again, this depends on the type of question, the type of response option, and the investigator's purpose. If the response options are bipolar, with one extreme indicating the opposite of the other (e.g., a strong positive versus a strong negative attitude), an odd number of responses permits equivocation (e.g., "neither agree nor disagree") or uncertainty (e.g., "not sure"); an even number usually does not. That is to say that an odd number implies a central "neutral" point (e.g., neither a positive nor a negative appraisal). An even number of responses, on the other hand, forces the respondent to make at least a weak commitment in the direction of one or the other extreme (e.g., a forced choice between a mildly positive or mildly negative appraisal as the least extreme response). Neither format is necessarily superior. The researcher may want to preclude equivocation if it is felt that subjects will select a neutral response as a means of avoiding a choice. In studies of social comparison choices, for example, the investigators may want to force subjects to express a preference for information about a more advantaged or less advantaged person. Consider these two alternative formats, the first of which was chosen for a study of social comparisons among people with arthritis (DeVellis, Holt, Renner, et al., 1990):

1. Would you prefer information about:
   (a) Patients who have worse arthritis than you have
   (b) Patients who have milder arthritis than you have
2. Would you prefer information about:
   (a) Patients who have worse arthritis than you have
   (b) Patients who have arthritis equally as bad as you have
   (c) Patients who have milder arthritis than you have

A neutral option such as 2b might permit unwanted equivocation. A neutral point may also be desirable. In a study assessing which of two risks (e.g., boredom versus danger) people prefer taking, a midpoint may be crucial. The researcher might vary the chance or severity of harm across several choices between a safe, dull activity and an exciting, risky one. The point at which a respondent is most nearly equivocal about risking the more exciting activity could then be used as an index of risk-taking:

Indicate your relative preference for activity A or activity B from the alternatives listed below by circling the appropriate phrase following the description of activity B.

Activity A: Reading a statistics book (no chance of severe injury)

1. Activity B: Taking a flight in a small commuter plane (very slight chance of severe injury)

| Strongly
Prefer A | Mildly
Prefer A | No
Preference | Mildly
Prefer B | Strongly
Prefer B |

2. Activity B: Taking a flight in a small open-cockpit plane (slight chance of severe injury)

Strongly	Mildly	No	Mildly	Strongly
Prefer A	Prefer A	Preference	Prefer B	Prefer B

3. Activity B: Parachute jumping from a plane with a backup chute (moderate chance of severe injury)

Strongly	Mildly	No	Mildly	Strongly
Prefer A	Prefer A	Preference	Prefer B	Prefer B

4. Activity B: Parachute jumping from a plane without a backup chute (substantial risk of severe injury)

Strongly	Mildly	No	Mildly	Strongly
Prefer A	Prefer A	Preference	Prefer B	Prefer B

5. Activity B: Jumping from a plane without a parachute and attempting to land on a soft target (almost certain severe injury)

Strongly	Mildly	No	Mildly	Strongly
Prefer A	Prefer A	Preference	Prefer B	Prefer B

The other merits or liabilities of this approach aside, it would clearly require that response options include a midpoint.

Specific types of response formats. Scale items occur in a dizzying variety of forms. However, there are several ways to present items that are used widely and have proven successful in diverse applications. Some of these are discussed below.

Likert scale. One of the most common item formats is a *Likert scale.* When a Likert scale is used, the item is presented as a declarative sentence, followed by response options that indicate varying degrees of agreement with or endorsement of the statement. (In fact, the preceding example of risk-taking used a Likert response format.) Depending on the phenomenon being investigated and the goals of the investigator, either an odd or even number of response options might accompany each statement. The response options should be worded so as to have roughly equal intervals with respect to agreement. That is to say the difference in agreement between any adjacent pair of responses should be about the same as for any other adjacent pair of response options. A common practice is to include six possible responses: strongly disagree, moderately disagree, mildly disagree, mildly agree, moderately agree, and strongly agree. These form a continuum from strong disagreement to strong agreement. A neutral midpoint can also be added. Common choices for a midpoint include neither agree nor disagree, and agree and disagree equally. There is legitimate room for discussion concerning the equivalence of these two midpoints. The first implies apathetic disinterest while the latter suggests strong but equal attraction to both agreement and disagreement. It may very well be that most respondents do not focus very much attention on subtleties of language but merely regard any reasonable response option in the center of the range as a midpoint irrespective of its precise wording.

Likert scaling is widely used in instruments measuring opinions, beliefs, and attitudes. It is often useful for these statements to be fairly (though not extremely) strong when used in a Likert format. Presumably, the moderation of opinion is expressed in the choice of response option. For example, the statements, "Physicians generally ignore what patients say," "Sometimes, physicians do not pay as much attention as they should to patients' comments," and, "Once in a while, physicians might forget or miss something a patient has told them" express strong, moderate, and weak opinions, respectively, concerning physicians' inattention to patients' remarks. Which is best for a Likert scale? Ultimately, of course, the one that most accurately reflects true differences of opinion is best. In choosing how strongly to word items in an initial item pool, the investigator might profitably ask, "How are people with different amounts or strengths of the attribute in question likely to respond?" In the case of the three examples just presented, the investigator might conclude that the last question would probably elicit strong agreement from people whose opinions fell along much of the continuum from positive to negative. If this conclusion proved correct, then the third statement would not do a good job of differentiating between people with strong versus moderate negative opinions.

In general, very mild statements may elicit too much agreement when used in Likert scales. Many people will strongly agree with such a statement as, "The safety and security of citizens is important." One could strongly agree with such a statement (i.e., choose an extreme response option) without holding an extreme opinion. Of course, the opposite is equally true. People holding any but the most extreme views might find themselves in disagreement with an extremely strong statement (for example, "Hunting down and punishing wrongdoers is more important than protecting the rights of individuals.") Of the two (overly mild or overly extreme) statements, the former may be the bigger problem for two reasons. First, our inclination is often to write statements that will not offend our subjects. Avoiding offensiveness is probably a good idea. However, it may lead us to favor items that nearly everyone will find agreeable. Another reason to be wary of items that are too mild is that they may represent the absence of belief or opinion. The third of our inattentive physician items in the preceding paragraph did not indicate the presence of a favorable attitude so much as the absence of an unfavorable one. Items of this sort may be poorly suited to the research goal because we are more often interested in the presence of some phenomenon rather than its absence.

In summary, a good Likert item should state the opinion, attitude, belief, or other construct under study in clear terms. It is neither necessary nor appropriate for this type of scale to span the range of weak to strong assertions of the construct. The response options provide the opportunity for gradations.

An example of items in Likert response formats is as follows:

1. Exercise is an essential component of a healthy life-style.

1	2	3	4	5	6
Strongly Disagree	Moderately Disagree	Mildly Disagree	Mildly Agree	Moderately Agree	Strongly Agree

2. Combating drug abuse should be a top national priority.

1	2	3	4	5
Completely True	Mostly True	Equally True and Untrue	Mostly Untrue	Completely Untrue

Semantic differential. The *semantic differential* scaling method is chiefly associated with the attitude research of Osgood and his colleagues (e.g., Osgood & Tannenbaum, 1955). Typically, a semantic differential is used in reference to one or more stimuli. In the case of attitudes, for example, the stimulus might be a group of people, such as automobile salesmen. Identification of the target stimulus is followed by a list of adjective pairs. Each pair represents opposite ends of a continuum, defined by adjectives (e.g., honest and dishonest). As shown in the example below, there are several lines between the adjectives that constitute the response options:

Automobile Salesmen

| Honest | __ __ __ __ __ __ __ | Dishonest |
| Quiet | __ __ __ __ __ __ __ | Noisy |

In essence, the individual lines (seven or nine are common numbers) represent points along the continuum defined by the adjectives. The respondent places a mark on one of the lines to indicate the point along the continuum that characterizes the stimulus. For example, if someone regarded auto salesmen as extremely dishonest, he or she might select the line closest to that adjective. Either extreme or moderate views can be expressed by choosing which line to mark. After rating the stimulus with regard to the first adjective pair, the person would proceed to additional adjective pairs separated by lines.

The adjectives one chooses can be either bipolar or unipolar, depending, as always, on the logic of the research questions the scale is intended to address. Bipolar adjectives each express the presence of opposite attributes, such as friendly and hostile. Unipolar adjective pairs indicate the presence and absence of a single attribute, such as friendly and not friendly.

Like the Likert scale, the semantic differential response format can be highly compatible with the theoretical models presented in the earlier chapters of this book. Sets of items can be written to tap the same underlying variable. For example, items using trustworthy/untrustworthy, fair/unfair, and truthful/untruthful as endpoints might be added to the first statement in the preceding example to constitute an "honesty" scale. Such a scale could be conceptualized as a set of items sharing a common latent variable (honesty) and conforming to the assumptions discussed in Chapter 2. Accordingly, the scores of the individual "honesty" items could be added and analyzed as described in a later section concerning the evaluation of items.

Visual analog. Another item format that is in some ways similar to the semantic differential is the *visual analog scale*. This response format presents the respondent with a continuous line between a pair of descriptors representing opposite ends of a continuum. The individual completing the item is instructed to place a mark at a point on the line that represents his or her opinion, experience, belief, or whatever is being measured. The visual analog scale, as the term "analog" in the name implies, is a continuous scale. The fineness of differentiation in assigning scores to points on the scale is determined by the investigator. Some of the advantages and disadvantages of a continuous response format were discussed earlier. An additional issue not raised at that time concerns possible differences in the interpretation of physical space as it relates to values on the continuum. A mark placed at a specific point along the line may not mean the same thing to different people even when the end points of the line are identically labeled for all respondents. Consider a visual analog scale for pain such as this:

No pain   The worst pain I
at all   _____   ever experienced

Does a response in the middle of the scale indicate pain about half of the time, constant pain of half the possible intensity, or something else entirely? Part of the problem with measuring pain is that pain can be evaluated on multiple dimensions, including frequency, intensity, and duration. Also, recollections of the worst pain a given person has ever experienced are likely to be distorted. Comparisons across individuals are further complicated by the fact that different people may have experienced different levels of "the worst pain." Of course, some of these problems reside with the phenomenon used in this example, pain, and not with the scale per se. However, the problem of idiosyncratic assignment of values along a visual analog scale can exist for other phenomena as well.

A major advantage of visual analog scales is that they are potentially very sensitive (Mayer, 1978). This can make them especially useful for measuring phenomena before and after some intervening event, such as an intervention or experimental manipulation, that exerts a relatively weak effect. A mild rebuke in the course of an experimental manipulation, for example, may not produce a shift on a 5-point measure of self-esteem. However, a subtle but systematic shift to lower values on a visual analog scale might occur among people in the "rebuke" condition of this hypothetical experiment. Sensitivity may be more advantageous when examining changes over time within the same individual rather than across individuals (Mayer, 1978). This may be so because, in the former case, there is no additional error due to extraneous differences between individuals.

Another potential advantage of visual analog scales when they are repeated over time is that it is difficult or impossible for subjects to encode their past responses with precision. To continue with the example from the preceding paragraph, a subject would probably have little difficulty remembering which of five numbered options to a self-esteem item he or she had previously chosen in response to a multi-response format such as a Likert scale. Unless one of the end points of a visual analog scale were chosen, however, it would be very difficult to recall precisely where a mark had been made along a featureless line. This could be advantageous if the investigator were concerned that respondents might be biased to appear consistent over time. Presumably, subjects motivated to be consistent would choose the same response after exposure to an experimental intervention as prior to such exposure. The visual analog format essentially rules out this possibility. If the post-manipulation responses departed consistently (i.e., usually in the same direction) from the pre-manipulation response for experimental subjects and randomly for controls, then the choice of a visual analog scale might have contributed to detecting a subtle phenomenon that other methods would have missed.

Visual analog scales have often been used as single-item measures. This has the sizeable disadvantage of precluding any determination of internal consistency. With a single-item measure, reliability can only be determined by the test-retest method described in Chapter 3 or by comparison with other measures of the same attribute having established psychometric properties. The former method suffers from the problems of test-retest assessments discussed earlier, notably the impossibility of differentiating instability of the measurement process from instability of the phenomenon being measured. The latter method is actually a construct validity comparison. However, because reliability is a necessary condition for validity, one can infer the reliability if validity is in evidence. Nonetheless, a better strategy may be to develop multiple visual analog items so that internal consistency can be determined.

Binary options. Another common response format gives subjects a choice between *binary options* for each item. The earlier examples of Thurstone and Guttman scales used binary options ("agree" and "disagree"), although scales with equally weighted items could also have binary response options. Subjects might, for example, be asked to check off all the adjectives on a list that they think apply to themselves. Or, they may be asked to answer "yes" or "no" to a list of emotional reactions they may have experienced in some specified situation. In both cases, responses reflecting items sharing a common latent variable (e.g., adjectives such as "sad," "unhappy," and "blue" representing depression) could be combined into a single score for that construct.

A major shortcoming of binary responses is that each item can have only minimal variability. Similarly, any pair of items can have only one of two levels of covariation: agreement or disagreement. Recall from Chapter 3 that the variance of a scale made up of multiple equally weighted items is exactly equal to the sum of all the elements in the covariance matrix for the individual items. With binary items, each item contributes precious little to that sum because of the limitations in possible variances and covariances. The practical consequence of this is that more items are needed to obtain the same degree of scale variance if the items are binary. However, binary items are usually extremely easy to answer. Therefore, the burden placed on the subject is very low for any one item. For example, most people can quickly decide whether certain adjectives are apt descriptions of themselves. As a result, subjects often are willing to complete more binary items than ones using a format demanding concentration on finer distinctions. Thus a binary format may allow the investigator to achieve adequate variation in scale scores by aggregating information over more items.

Item time frames. Another issue that pertains to the formatting of items is the time frame specified or implied. Kelly and McGrath (1988), in another volume in this series, have discussed the importance of considering the temporal features of different measures. Some scales will not make reference to a time frame, implying a universal time perspective. Locus of control scales, for example, often contain items that imply an enduring belief about causality. Items such as "If I take the right actions I can stay healthy" (Wallston et al., 1978) presume that this belief is relatively stable. This is consistent with the theoretical characterization of locus of control as a generalized rather than specific expectancy for control over outcomes (although there has been a shift toward greater specificity in more recent measures of locus of control beliefs—e. g., DeVellis, DeVellis, Revicki, Lurie, Runyan, & Bristol, 1985). Other measures assess relatively transient phenomena. Depression, for example, can vary over time and scales to measure it have acknowledged this point (Mayer, 1978). For example, the widely used Center for Epidemiological Studies Depression (CES-D) scale (Radloff, 1977) uses a format that asks respondents to indicate how often during the past week they have experienced various mood states. Some measures, such as anxiety scales (e.g., Spielberger, Gorsuch, & Lushene, 1970), are developed in different forms intended to assess relatively transient states or relatively enduring traits (Zuckerman, 1983). The investigator should choose a time frame for a scale actively rather than passively. Theory is an important guide to this process. Is the phenomenon of interest a fundamental and enduring aspect of individuals' personalities, or is it likely to be dependent on changing circumstances? Is the scale intended to detect subtle variations occurring over a brief time frame (e.g., increases in negative affect after viewing a sad movie) or changes that may evolve over a lifetime (e.g., progressive political conservatism with increasing age)?

In conclusion, the item formats, including response options and instructions, should reflect the nature of the latent variable of interest and the intended uses of the scale.

STEP 4:
HAVE INITIAL ITEM POOL
REVIEWED BY EXPERTS

Thus far, we have discussed the need for clearly articulating what the phenomenon of interest is, generating a pool of suitable items, and selecting a response format for those items. The next step in the process is having a group of people who are knowledgeable in the content area review the item pool. This review serves multiple purposes related to maximizing the content validity (see Chapter 4) of the scale.

First, having experts review your item pool can confirm or invalidate your definition of the phenomenon. You can ask your panel of experts (e.g., colleagues who have worked extensively with the construct in question or related phenomena) to rate *how relevant they think each item is to what you intend to measure*. This is especially useful if you are developing a measure that will consist of separate scales to measure multiple constructs. If you have been careful in developing your items, then experts should have little trouble determining which items correspond to which constructs. In essence, your thoughts about what each item measures is the hypothesis, and the responses of the experts are the confirming or disconfirming data. Even if all the items are intended to tap a single attribute or construct, expert review is useful. If experts read something into an item you did not plan to include, subjects completing a final scale might do likewise.

The mechanics of obtaining evaluations of item relevance usually involve providing the expert panel with your working definition of the construct. They are then asked to rate each item with respect to its relevance vis-à-vis the construct as you have defined it. This might entail merely rating relevance as high, moderate, or low for each item. In addition, you might invite your experts to comment on individual items as they see fit. This makes their job a bit more difficult but can yield excellent information. A few insightful comments about why certain items are ambiguous, for example, might give you a new perspective on how you have attempted to measure the construct.

Reviewers also can *evaluate the items' clarity and conciseness.* The content of an item may be relevant to the construct, but its wording may be problematic. This bears on item reliability because an ambiguous or otherwise unclear item, to a greater degree than a clear item, can reflect factors extraneous to the latent variable. In your instructions to reviewers, ask them to point out awkward or confusing items and suggest alternative wordings, if they are so inclined.

A third service that your expert reviewers can provide is *pointing out ways of tapping the phenomenon that you have failed to include.* There may be a whole approach that you have overlooked. For example, you may have included many items referring to illness in a pool of items concerned with health beliefs but failed to consider injury as another relevant departure from health. By reviewing the variety of ways you have captured the phenomenon of interest, your reviewers can help you to maximize the content validity of your scale.

A final word of caution concerning expert opinion: The final decision to accept or reject the advice of your experts is your responsibility as the scale developer. Sometimes content experts might not understand the principles of scale construction. This can lead to bad advice. A recommendation I have frequently encountered from colleagues without scale development experience is to eliminate items that concern the same thing. As discussed earlier, removing all redundancy from an item pool or a final scale would be a grave error because redundancy is an integral aspect of internal consistency. However, this comment might indicate that the wording, vocabulary, and sentence structure of the items are too similar and could be improved. Pay careful attention to all the suggestions you receive from content experts. Then make your own informed decisions about how to use their advice.

At this point in the process, the scale developer has a set of items that has been reviewed by experts and modified accordingly. It is now time to advance to the next step.

STEP 5:
CONSIDER INCLUSION OF
VALIDATION ITEMS

Obviously, the heart of the scale development questionnaire is the set of items from which the scale under development will emerge. However, some foresight can pay off handsomely. It might be possible and relatively convenient to include some additional items in the same questionnaire that will help in determining the validity of the final scale. There are at least two types of items to consider.

The first type of item a scale developer might choose to include in a questionnaire serves to detect flaws or problems. Respondents might not be answering the items of primary interest for the reasons you assume. There may be other motivations influencing their responses. Learning this early is advantageous. One type of motivation that can be assessed fairly easily is *social desirability*. If an individual is strongly motivated to present herself or himself in a way that society regards as positive, item responses may be distorted. Including a social desirability scale allows the investigator to assess how strongly individual items are influenced by social desirability. Items that correlate substantially with the social desirability score obtained should be considered as candidates for exclusion unless there is a sound theoretical reason that indicates otherwise. A brief and useful social desirability scale has been developed by Strahan and Gerbasi (1972). This 10-item measure can be conveniently inserted into a questionnaire.

There are other sources of items for detecting undesirable response tendencies (Anastasi, 1968). The Minnesota Multiphasic Personality Inventory, or MMPI (Hathaway & Meehl, 1951; Hathaway & McKinley, 1967), includes several scales aimed at detecting various response biases. In some instances, it may be appropriate to include these types of scales.

The other class of items to consider including at this stage pertain, to the construct validity of the scale. As discussed in Chapter 4, if theory asserts that the phenomenon you are setting out to measure relates to other constructs, then the performance of the scale vis-à-vis measures of those other constructs can serve as evidence of its validity. Rather than mounting a separate validation effort after constituting the final scale, it may be possible to include measures of relevant constructs at this stage. The resultant pattern of relationships can provide support for claims of validity or, alternatively, provide clues if the set of items does not perform as anticipated.

STEP 6:
ADMINISTER ITEMS TO A
DEVELOPMENT SAMPLE

After deciding which construct-related and validity items to include in your questionnaire, you must administer them, along with the pool of new items, to some subjects. The sample of subjects should be large. How large is large? It is difficult to find a consensus on this issue. Let us examine the rationale for a large sample. Nunnally (1978) points out that the primary sampling issue in scale development involves the sampling of items from a hypothetical universe (cf. Ghiselli et al., 1981). In order to concentrate on the adequacy of the items, the sample should be sufficiently large to eliminate subject variance as a significant concern. He suggests that 300 people is an adequate number. However, practical experience suggests that scales have been successfully developed with smaller samples. The number of items and the number of scales to be extracted also have a bearing on the sample size issue. If only a single scale is to be extracted from a pool of about 20 items, fewer than 300 subjects might suffice.

There are several risks in using too few subjects. First, the patterns of covariation among the items may not be stable. An item that appears to increase internal consistency may turn out to be a dud when it is used on a separate sample. If items are selected for inclusion (as they very well may be) on the basis of their contribution to alpha, having a small developmental sample can paint an inaccurately rosy picture of internal consistency. When the ratio of subjects to items is relatively low and the sample size is not large, the correlations among items can be influenced by chance to a fairly substantial degree. When a scale whose items were selected under these conditions is readministered, the chance factors that made certain items look good initially are no longer operative. Consequently, the alpha obtained on occasions other than the initial development study may be lower than expected. Similarly, a potentially good item may be excluded because its correlation with other items was attenuated purely by chance.

A second potential pitfall of small sample size is that the development sample may not represent the population for which the scale is intended. Of course, this can also be the case if the development sample is large, but a small sample is even more likely to exclude certain types of individuals. Thus a scale developer should consider both the size and composition of the development sample. A careful investigator might choose to address the generalizability of a scale across populations (or some other facet) by a G-study, as discussed in Chapter 3.

Not all types of nonrepresentativeness are identical. There are at least two different ways in which a sample may not be representative of the larger population. The first involves the level of attribute present in the sample versus the intended population. For example, a sample might represent a narrower range of the attribute than would be expected of the population. This constriction of range may also be asymmetrical, so that the mean score obtained on the scale for the sample is appreciably higher or lower than one would expect for the population. Opinions regarding the appropriate legal drinking age, for example, might very well differ on a college campus than in a community at large. A mean value of the attribute that is not representative does not necessarily disqualify the sample for purposes of scale development. It may yield inaccurate expectations for scale means while still providing an accurate picture of the internal consistency the scale possesses. For example, a sample of this sort might still lead to correct conclusions about which items are most strongly interrelated.

A more troublesome type of sample nonrepresentativeness involves a sample that is qualitatively rather than quantitatively different from the target population. Specifically, a sample in which the relationships among items or constructs may differ from the population is reason for concern. If a sample is quite unusual, items may have a different meaning than for people in general. The patterns of association among items might reflect unusual attributes shared among sample members but rare in the broader community. In other words, the groupings of interrelated items that emerge (e.g., from a factor analysis) may be atypical. Stated a bit more formally, the underlying causal structure relating variables to true scores may be different if a sample is unlike the population in important ways. Consider some rather obvious examples: If the members of the sample chosen do not understand a key word that recurs among the items and has relevance to the construct, their responses may tell little or nothing about how the scale would perform under different circumstances. The word "sick" means "ill" in the United States but "nauseated" (i.e., sick to one's stomach) in England. A set of questions about illness developed for one group may have a markedly different meaning for the other. If the scale concerns a specific health problem not usually associated with nausea (e.g., arthritis), items that use the word "ill" might cluster together because of their distinct meaning if the sample were British. An American sample, on the other hand, would be unlikely to differentiate statements about being ill from other health-related items. Even within the United States, the same word can have different meanings. Among rural Southerners, for example, "bad blood" is sometimes used as a euphemism for venereal disease, whereas in other parts of the country it means animosity. If an item discussing "bad blood between relatives" performed differently among a sample of rural Southern versus other samples, it would hardly be surprising.

The consequences of this second type of sample nonrepresentativeness can severely harm a scale development effort. The underlying structure that emerges—the patterns of covariation among items that are so important to issues of scale reliability—may be a quirk of the sample used in development. If a researcher has reason to believe that the meaning

ascribed to items may be atypical among a development sample, great
caution should be used in interpreting the findings obtained from that
sample.

STEP 7:
EVALUATE THE ITEMS

After an initial pool of items has been developed, scrutinized, and
administered to an appropriately large and representative sample, it is
time to evaluate the performance of the individual items so that appropriate ones can be identified to constitute the scale. This is, in many ways,
the heart of the scale development process. Item evaluation is second
perhaps only to item development in its importance.

Initial examination of items' performance. When discussing item development, we referred to some of the qualities that are desirable in a scale
item. Let us reconsider that issue. The ultimate quality we seek in an item
is a high correlation with the true score of the latent variable. This follows
directly from the discussion of reliability in Chapter 3. We cannot directly
assess the true score (if we could, we probably would not need a scale)
and thus cannot directly compute its correlations with items. However,
we can make inferences, based on the formal measurement models that
have been discussed thus far. When discussing parallel tests in Chapter 2,
I noted that the correlation between any two items equaled the square of
the correlation between either item and the true score. This squared value
is the reliability of each of the items. So, we can learn about relationships
to true scores from correlations among items. The higher the correlations
among items, the higher are the individual item reliabilities (i.e., the more
intimately they are related to the true score). The more reliable the
individual items are, the more reliable will be the scale that they comprise
(assuming that they share a common latent variable). So, the first quality
we seek in a set of scale items is that they be *highly intercorrelated.* One
way to determine how intercorrelated the items are is to inspect the
correlation matrix.

Reverse scoring. If there are items whose correlations with other items
are negative, then the appropriateness of *reverse scoring* those items
should be considered. Sometimes, when generating items, we think of
statements that relate equally to the construct, but some may be positiv

and others negative "I am happy" and "I am sad" both pertain to affect. However, they are opposites. If we wanted high scores on our scale to measure happiness, then we would have to ascribe a high value to endorsing the "happy" item but a low value to endorsing the "sad" item. That is to say, we would reverse-score the sadness item. Sometimes, items are administered in such a way that they are already reversed. For example, subjects might be asked to circle higher numerical values to indicate agreement with a "happy" item and lower values to endorse a "sad" one. One way to do this is by having the verbal descriptors for the response options (e.g., "strongly disagree," "moderately disagree," etc.) always be in the same order for all items, but having the numbers associated with them either ascend or descend, depending on the item:

1. I am sad often.

6	5	4	3	2	1
Strongly Disagree	Moderately Disagree	Mildly Disagree	Mildly Agree	Moderately Agree	Strongly Agree

2. Much of the time, I am happy.

1	2	3	4	5	6
Strongly Disagree	Moderately Disagree	Mildly Disagree	Mildly Agree	Moderately Agree	Strongly Agree

This process may confuse the subject. People may ignore the words after realizing that they are the same for all items. However, it is probably preferable to altering the order of the descriptors (e.g., from "strongly disagree to "strongly agree, from left to right, for some items and the reverse for others). Another option is to have both the verbal descriptions and their corresponding numbers the same for all items but to enter different values for certain items at the time of data coding. Changing scores for certain items at the time of coding is both tedious and potentially error prone. For every subject, every item to be reverse-scored must be given the special attention involved in reverse scoring. This creates numerous opportunities for mistakes.

The easiest method for reverse scoring is to do so electronically once the data have been entered into a computer. A few computer statements can handle all the reverse scoring for all subjects' data. If the response options have numerical values and the desired transformation is to reverse the order of values, a simple formula can be used. For example, assume that a set of mood items formatted using a Likert scale was scored from 1 to 7, with higher numbers indicating agreement. Assume further that, for ease of comprehension, both positive mood and negative mood items used this same response format. However, if endorsing positive mood items is assigned a high score, then the scale is essentially a positive mood scale. Endorsing a positive mood item should result in a high value, and endorsing a negative mood item should yield a low value. This is what would be obtained if, for all negative mood items, responses of 7 were changed to 1, 6 to 2, and so forth. This type of transformation can be accomplished by creating a new score from the old score with the following formula: NEW = $(J + 1)$ - OLD, where NEW and OLD refer to the transformed and original scores, respectively, and J is the original number of response options. In the example presented, J would equal 7 and $(J + 1)$ would be 8. Subtracting a score of 7 from 8 would yield 1, subtracting 6 would yield 2, and so forth.

Some negative correlations among items may not be correctable by reverse scoring items. For example, reverse scoring a given item might eliminate some negative correlations but create others. This usually indicates that some of the items simply do not belong because they are not consistently related to other items. Any item that is positively correlated with some and negatively correlated with others in a homogeneous set should be eliminated if no pattern of reverse scoring items eliminates the negative correlations.

Item-scale correlations. If we want to arrive at a set of highly intercorrelated items, then each individual item should correlate substantially with the collection of remaining items. We can examine this property for each item by computing its *item-scale correlation.* There are two types of item-scale correlation. The corrected item-scale correlation correlates the item being evaluated with all the scale items, excluding itself, while the uncorrected item-scale correlation correlates the item in question with the entire set of candidate items, including itself. If there were 10 items being considered for a scale, the corrected item-scale correlation for any one of the 10 items would consist of its correlation with the other nine. The uncorrected correlation would consist of its correlation with all ten. In theory, the uncorrected value tells us how representative the item is of the whole scale. This is analogous, for example, to correlating one subset of an IQ test with the entire test to determine if the subscale is a suitable proxy. However, although an uncorrected item-total correlation makes good conceptual sense, the reality is that the item's inclusion in the "scale" can inflate the correlation coefficient. The fewer the number of items in the set, the bigger the difference that inclusion or exclusion of the item under scrutiny will make. In general, it is probably advisable to examine the corrected item-total correlation. An item with a high value for this correlation is more desirable than an item with a low value.

Item variances. Another valuable attribute for a scale item is *relatively high variance.* To take an extreme case, if all individuals answer a given item identically, it will not discriminate at all among individuals with different levels of the construct being measured, and its variance would be 0. In contrast, if the development sample is diverse, then the range of scores obtained for an item should be diverse as well. This implies a fairly high variance.

Item means. A mean *close to the center of the range* of possible scores is also desirable. If, for example, the response options for each item ranged from 1, corresponding to "strongly disagree," to 7, for "strongly agree," an item mean near 4 would be ideal. If a mean were near one of the extremes of the range, then the item might fail to detect certain values of the construct. A piling up of scores at the value 7, for example, would suggest that the item was not worded strongly enough (i.e., that it was rare to find anyone who would disagree with it).

Generally, items with means too near to an extreme of the response range will have low variances, and those that vary over a narrow range will correlate poorly with other items. As stated previously, an item that does not vary cannot covary. Thus either a lopsided mean or a low variance for any reason will tend to reduce an item's correlation with other items. As a result, you can usually concentrate primarily on the pattern of correlations among items as a gauge of their potential value. Inspecting means and variances, however, is a useful double-check once a tentative selection of items has been made on the basis of the correlations.

Coefficient alpha. One of the most important indicators of a scale's quality is the reliability coefficient, alpha. Virtually all the item problems discussed thus far—a noncentral mean, poor variability, negative correlations among items, low item-scale correlations, and weak inter-item correlations—will tend to reduce alpha. Therefore, after we have selected our items, weeding out the poor ones and retaining the good ones, alpha is one way of evaluating how successful we have been. Alpha is an indication of the proportion of variance in the scale scores that is attributable to the true score.

There are several options for computing alpha, differing in degree of automation. Some computer packages have item analysis programs that compute alpha. In SPSS-X, the RELIABILITY procedure computes alpha for a full scale and for all $k - 1$ versions (i.e., every possible version with a single item removed). The program also provides corrected and uncorrected item-scale correlations. SAS-PC (Version 6.03) includes alpha calculations as a feature of the correlation program, PROC CORR. By including the option ALPHA in the PROC CORR statement, the variables listed in the VAR statement will be treated as a scale and alpha will be computed for the full set of items as well as all possible $k - 1$ item sets. Item-scale correlations are also provided. As of this writing, current mainframe versions of SAS do not include the ALPHA option. Perhaps the simplest means of computing alpha in this instance is to begin by creating a variable that is the sum of the individual scale items (after reverse-scoring items as appropriate). You can then use PROC MEANS to generate the standard deviations for the individual items and for the new variable representing the scale as a whole. Those values, plus the number of items, k, can be entered into the covariance-based alpha formula presented in Chapter 3:

$$\alpha = \frac{k}{k - 1} \left(1 - \frac{\Sigma \sigma_i^2}{\sigma_{yi}^2} \right)$$

Alternatively, one can generate a covariance matrix from PROC CORR. The sum of values along the main diagonal equals the numerator of the right-hand term in the above formula, and the sum of all elements in the covariance matrix equals the denominator. An advantage of computing alpha from a covariance matrix (assuming that you do not have access to a package that will provide alpha directly) is that the effect of deleting certain items can be determined easily. To determine the effect of deleting any item, merely draw a line through the row and column of the matrix corresponding to the item (e.g., the third row and third column if the third variable is to be deleted). You can then compute the numerator by summing the diagonal values minus the one crossed out and the denominator by summing all of the elements except those that are crossed out. Of course, you could just as easily eliminate several items at once by crossing out multiple rows and columns and working with the remaining values.

A final option for computing alpha is to use the Spearman-Brown formula, which was introduced in Chapter 3. This formula uses information available from a correlation matrix rather than a covariance matrix as the basis for computing alpha. A shortcoming of this approach is that correlations are standardized covariances and standardizing the individual items might affect the value of alpha. If one adheres strictly to the model of parallel tests, then this is inconsequential because the correlations are assumed to be equal. However, they virtually never are exactly equal. The essentially tau-equivalent tests model does not require equal correlations among items, only equal covariances. Thus the proportion of each individual item's variance that is due to error is free to vary under that model. However, because the Spearman-Brown formula actually works with *average* inter-item correlations and, as one of the implications of the tau-equivalent model is that the average item-scale correlations are equal for each item, there is still no problem. Nonetheless, there can be small (but sometimes large) differences between the values of alpha obtained from covariance-based versus correlation-based computational methods. Because the covariance matrix uses the data in a purer form (without standardization), it is preferred and should generally be used.

Theoretically, alpha can take on values from 0.0 to 1.0, although it is unlikely that it will attain either of these extreme values. If alpha is negative, something is wrong. A likely problem is negative correlations (or covariances) among the items. If this occurs, try reverse scoring or deleting items as described earlier in this chapter. Nunnally (1978) suggests a value of .70 as a lower acceptable bound for alpha. It is not unusual to see published scales with lower alphas. Different methodologists and investigators begin to squirm at different levels of alpha. My personal comfort ranges for research scales are as follows: below .60, unacceptable; between .60 and .65, undesirable; between .65 and .70, minimally acceptable; between .70 and .80, respectable; between .80 and .90, very good; much above .90, one should consider shortening the scale (see following section). I should emphasize that these are *personal and subjective* groupings of alpha values. I cannot defend them on strictly rational grounds. However, they reflect my experience and seem to overlap substantially with other investigators' appraisals. The values I have suggested apply to *stable* alphas. During development, items are selected, either directly or indirectly, on the basis of their contribution to alpha. Some of the apparent covariation among items may be due to chance. Therefore, it is advisable during the development stage to strive for alphas that are a bit higher than you would like. Then, if the alphas deteriorate somewhat when used in a new research context, they will still be acceptably high. As noted earlier, if the developmental sample is small, the investigator should be especially concerned that the initial alpha estimates obtained during scale development may not be stable. As we shall see, this is also the case when the number of items making up the scale is small. A situation in which the suggested "comfort ranges" for alpha do not apply is when one is developing a scale that requires critical accuracy. Clinical situations are an example. The suggested guidelines are suitable for *research instruments* that will be used with *group data*. For example, a scale with an alpha of .85 is probably perfectly adequate for use in a study comparing groups with respect to the construct being measured. Individual assessment, especially when important decisions rest on that assessment, demand a much higher standard. Scales that are intended for individual diagnostic, employment, academic placement, or other important purposes should probably have considerably higher reliabilities, in the mid-.90s, for example.

In some situations, such as when a scale consists of a single item, it will be impossible to use alpha as the index of reliability. If possible, some reliability assessment should be made. Test-retest correlation may be the only option in the single-item instance. Although this index of reliability is imperfect, as discussed in Chapter 3, it is clearly better than no reliability assessment at all. A preferable alternative, if possible, would be to constitute the scale using more than a single item.

STEP 8:
OPTIMIZE SCALE LENGTH

Effect of scale length on reliability. At this stage of the scale development process, the investigator has a pool of items that demonstrate acceptable reliability. A scale's alpha is influenced by two characteristics: the extent of covariation among the items and the number of items in the scale. For items that have item-scale correlations about equal to the *average* inter-item correlation (i.e., items that are fairly typical), adding more will increase alpha and removing more will lower it. Generally, shorter scales are good because they place less of a burden on respondents. Longer scales, on the other hand, are good because they tend to be more reliable. Obviously, maximizing one of these assets reduces the other. Therefore, the scale developer should give some thought to the optimal trade-off between brevity and reliability.

If a scale's reliability is too low, then brevity is no virtue. Subjects may, indeed, be more willing to answer a 3-item than a 10-item scale. However, if the researcher cannot assign any meaning to the scores obtained from the shorter version, then nothing has been gained. Thus the issue of trading off reliability for brevity should be confined to situations when the researcher has "reliability to spare." When this is, in fact, the case, it may be appropriate to buy a shorter scale at the price of a bit less reliability.

Effects of dropping "bad" items. Whether dropping "bad" items actually increases or slightly lowers alpha depends on just how poor the items are that will be dropped, and on the number of items in the scale. Consider the effect of more or fewer items that are equally "good" items—i.e., that have comparable correlations with their counterparts: With fewer items, a greater change in alpha results from the addition or subtraction of each item. If the average interitem correlation among four items is .50, the alpha will equal .80. If there are only three items with an average interitem correlation of .50, alpha drops to .75. Five items with the same average correlation would have an alpha of .83. For 9-, 10-, and 11-item scales with average interitem correlations of .50, alphas would be .90, .91, and .92, respectively. In the latter instances, the alphas are not only higher, but they are much closer in value to one another.

If an item has a sufficiently lower-than-average correlation with the other items, dropping it will raise alpha. If its average correlation with the other items is only slightly below (or equal to, or above) the overall average, then retaining the item will increase alpha. I stated above that a 4-item scale would attain an alpha of .80, with an average inter-item correlation of .50. How low would the average correlation of one item to the other three have to be for that item's elimination to help rather than hurt alpha? First, consider what the average inter-item correlation would have to be for a 3-item scale to achieve an alpha of .80. It would need to be .57. So, after eliminating the worst of four items, the remaining three would need an average inter-item correlation of .57 for alpha to hold its value of .80. Three items whose average inter-item correlation was lower than .57 would have a lower alpha than four items whose inter-item correlations averaged .50. Assuming that the three best items of a 4-item scale had an average correlation among them of .57, the average correlation between the remaining (and thus worst) item and the other three would have to be lower than .43 for its elimination to actually increase alpha. (Having three items whose intercorrelations average .57 and one whose average correlation with the other three is .43 yields an overall average inter-item correlation among the four of .50.) For any value larger than .43, having a fourth item does more good than lowering the average inter-item correlation does harm. Thus the one "bad" item would have to be a fair bit worse than the other three $(.57 - .43 = .14)$ to be worth eliminating.

Now, consider the situation when there is a 10-item scale with an alpha = .80. First of all, the average inter-item correlation need only be about .29, illustrating the manner in which more items offset weaker correlations among them. For a 9-item scale to achieve the same alpha, the average inter-item correlation would need to be about .31. A "bad" item would need to have an average inter-item correlation with the remaining nine items of about .20 or less in order for its inclusion as a tenth item to pull the overall average inter-item correlation below .29. A failure to bring the average below this value would result in the item's inclusion benefiting alpha. The average inter-item correlation difference between the nine "good" items and the one "bad" in this case is $.31 - .20 = .11$, a smaller difference than the one found in the 4-item example.

Tinkering with scale length. How does one go about "tinkering" with scale length in practice? Obviously, items that contribute least to the overall internal consistency should be the first to be considered for exclusion. These can be identified in a number of ways. The SPSS-X RELIABILITY procedure and the ALPHA option of PROC CORR in SAS-PC show what the effect of omitting each item would be on the overall alpha. The items whose omission has the least negative or most positive effect on alpha is usually the best one to drop first. The item-scale correlations can also be used as a barometer of which items are expendable. Those with the lowest item-scale correlations should be eliminated first. SPSS-X also provides a squared multiple correlation for each item, obtained by regressing the item on all of the remaining items. This is an estimate of the item's *communality,* the extent to which the item shares variance with the other items. As with item-scale correlations, items with the lowest squared multiple correlations should be the prime candidates for exclusion. Generally, these various indices of item quality converge. A poor item-scale correlation is typically accompanied by a low squared multiple correlation and a small loss, or even a gain, in alpha when the item is eliminated. Scale length affects the precision of alpha. In practice, a computed alpha is an estimate of reliability dependent on the appropriateness of the measurement assumptions to the actual data. It has already been noted that alpha increases when more items are included (unless they are relatively poor items). In addition, the *reliability of alpha as an estimate of reliability* increases with the number of items. This means that an alpha computed for a longer scale will have a narrower confidence interval around it than will an alpha computed for a shorter scale. Across administrations, a longer scale will yield more similar values for alpha than will a shorter one. This fact should be considered in deciding how long or short to make a scale during development. Finally, it is important to remember that a margin of safety should be built into alpha when trying to optimize scale length. Alpha may decrease somewhat when the scale is administered to a sample other than the one used for its development.

Split samples. If the development sample is sufficiently large, it may be possible to split it into two subsamples. One can serve as the primary development sample, and the other can be used to cross-validate the findings. So, for example, data from the first subsample can be used to compute alphas, evaluate items, tinker with scale length, and arrive at a final version of the scale that seems optimal. The second subsample can then be used to replicate these findings. The choice of items to retain will not have been based at all on the second subsample. Thus alphas and other statistics computed for this group would not manifest the chance effects, such as alpha inflation, that was discussed earlier. If the alphas remain fairly constant across the two subsamples, you can be more comfortable assuming that these values are not distorted by chance. Of course, the two subsamples are likely to be much more similar than two totally different samples. The subsamples, divided randomly from the entire development sample, are likely to represent the same population; in contrast, an entirely new sample might represent a slightly different population. Also, data collection periods for the two subsamples are not separated by time whereas a development sample and a totally separate sample almost always are. Furthermore, any special conditions that may have applied to data collection for one subsample would apply equally to the other. Examples of special conditions include exposure to specific research personnel, physical settings, and clarity of questionnaire printing. Also, the two subsamples may be the only two groups to complete the scale items together with all of the items from the original pool that were eventually rejected. If rejected items exercised any effects on the responses to the scale items, these would be comparable for both subsamples.

Despite the unique similarity of the resultant subsamples, replicating findings by splitting the developmental sample provides valuable information about scale stability. The two subsamples differ in one key aspect: In the case of the first subsample on whose data item selection was based, the opportunity existed for unstable, chance factors to be confused with reliable covariation among items. No such opportunity for systematically attributing chance results to reliability exist for the second group because its data did not influence item selection. This crucial difference is sufficient reason to value the information that sample splitting can offer. The most obvious way to split a sufficiently large sample is to halve it. However, if the sample is too small to yield adequately large halves, you can split unevenly. The larger subsample can be used for the more crucial process of item evaluation and scale construction and the smaller for cross-validation.

EXERCISES

Assume that you are developing a fear-of-snakes measure, having a 6-choice Likert response format, using 300 subjects. Although more items would be desirable for actual scale development, for these exercises:

1. Generate a pool of 10 Likert-format items.
2. Estimate, for each item you have written, what Likert scale values would be endorsed by the "average person" (i.e., neither a snake phobic nor a snake charmer).
3. Pick an item from the pool that you suspect might elicit an extreme response from an average person and rewrite it to elicit a more moderate response.
4. Generate another 10 Likert items to tap a construct *other than* fear of snakes. Randomly mix these items with the original 10 and ask a few friends to indicate what they think each of the items is intended to measure.
5. Using either fear of snakes or the construct underlying your second pool of 10 items, list directly observable behaviors that could be used to validate a scale measuring that construct and explain how you could use behavioral data for validation.
7. What would the alpha for the scale be if your 10 fear-of snakes items had an average inter-item correlation of .30?[1]
8. How could you use split samples to estimate and cross-validate the scale's coefficient alpha?

NOTE

1. For Exercise 7, alpha = $[10 * .30] / [1 + (9 * .30)] = .81$.

6

Factor Analytic Strategies

When discussing different theoretical models that could be used to describe the relationship of a scale's items to the latent variable (see Chapter 2), I briefly mentioned the general factor model. It is a model that does not assume that only one latent variable is the source of all covariation among the items. Instead, that model allows multiple latent variables to serve as causes of variation in a set of items.

To illustrate how more than one latent variable might underlie a set of items, I will describe a specific, albeit hypothetical, situation. Many constructs of interest to us as social scientists can be operationalized at multiple levels of specificity. The terms *psychological adjustment, moods, negative affect, anxiety*, and *test anxiety* are examples of hierarchical phenomena. Each term could subsume those that follow it in the list, and it might be possible to develop measures at each level of specificity. Presumably, differently worded items could tap either a specific, middling, or general level of this continuum.

Let us make this example a bit more specific and consider a set of 25 items that all pertain to affect. Our concern is whether these items should make up one or many scales. Perhaps all the items belong together. Or, it might be better to have separate scales for different mood states, such as depression, euphoria, hostility, anxiety, and so on. Maybe it would be even better to split the positive and negative affect items (e.g., "happy" versus "sad" for depression or "tense" versus "calm" for anxiety) into separate scales. How do we know what is best? Essentially, the question is, do a set of items asking about several mood states have one or many latent variables underlying them?

Attempting to answer these questions using only the methods discussed in the preceding chapters would be daunting. We could compute alpha on the entire set of mood items. Alpha would tell us something about how much variance the items had in common. If alpha were low, we might search for subsets of items correlating more strongly with each other. For example, we might suspect that positive and negative affect items do not correlate with one another and that combining them was lowering alpha. The alphas for these more homogenous (all positive or all negative affect) subsets of items should be higher. We might then speculate that even more homogenous subsets (e.g., separating anxiety from depression in addition to positive from negative) should have still higher alphas. However, we might also worry that these more specific and homogenous scales would correlate strongly with each other because they were merely tapping different aspects of the same affective state. This would suggest that their items belonged in the same rather than in separate scales.

It should be emphasized that a relatively high alpha is no guarantee that all the items reflect the influence of a single latent variable. If a scale consisted of 25 items, 12 reflecting primarily one latent variable and the remaining 13 primarily another, the correlation matrix for all the items should have some high and some low values. Correlations based on two items representing primarily the same latent variable should be high, and those based on items primarily influenced by different latent variables should be relatively low. However, the *average* inter-item correlation might be high enough to yield a respectable alpha for a 25-item scale (it need be only .14 to yield an alpha of .80, for example).

Factor analysis, the topic of this chapter, is a useful analytic tool that can tell us, in a way that reliability coefficients cannot, about important properties of a scale. It can help us determine *empirically* how many constructs, or latent variables, or *factors* underlie a set of items.

OVERVIEW OF FACTOR ANALYSIS

Factor analysis serves several related purposes. One of its primary functions is to help an investigator determine *how many latent variables* underlie a set of items (or other variables). Thus in the case of the 25 affect items, factor analysis could help the investigator determine whether one broad or several more specific constructs were needed to characterize the item set. A second purpose, which follows from the first, is to provide a means of explaining variation among relatively many original variables (e.g., 25 items) using relatively few newly created variables (i.e., the factors). This amounts to *condensing* information so that variation can be accounted for by using a smaller number of variables. For example, instead of needing 25 scores to describe how respondents answered the items, it might be possible to compute fewer scores (perhaps even one) based on combining items. A third purpose is to *define the substantive content or meaning of the factors* (i.e., latent variables) that account for the variation among a larger set of items. This is accomplished by identifying groups of items that covary with one another and appear to define meaningful underlying latent variables. If, say, two factors emerged from an analysis of the 25 affect items, the individual items making up those factor groupings could provide a clue as to what were the underlying latent variables represented by the factors.

The following sections present a conceptual summary of factor analysis. Readers who want a more thorough treatment of factor analysis should consult a text devoted to the topic, such as Cureton, 1983; Gorsuch 1983; Harman, 1976; or McDonald, 1984.

Starting from a covariance matrix. The analysis typically begins by constructing a covariance (or correlation) matrix from the data submitted to a factor analytic program. This matrix is made up of diagonal elements that are the variances of the individual items (or unities, in the case of a correlation matrix) and off-diagonal elements that are the covariances (or correlations) between all item pairs. The values along the diagonal may be simple variances (or unities) or estimates that are corrected for error, depending on the type of factor analysis performed. We will assume that the uncorrected values are used. Recall from our earlier discussion of covariance matrices that it is possible to partition the total variance among the items into the portion that is shared (i.e., the covariances), and the portion that is unique (i.e., the variances). The shared and unique components of a covariance matrix can be represented diagrammatically. A diagram showing 25 items would be extremely difficult to interpret, so let us simplify things. In Figure 6.1, three items, A, B, and C, are represented as boxes and their covariation with one another is shown as areas that overlap. The cross-hashed area represents the covariation shared among all three items. The areas marked by dots represent covariation between pairs of items. The unshaded area is the unique, unshared portion of the individual items. Recalling the covariance matrix, the unshaded portions of our figure would contribute to the item variances running along the diagonal of the matrix but not to any of the off-diagonal covariances. Because both the dotted and cross-hashed areas represent shared variance, they correspond to information in the off-diagonal elements of the covariance matrix.

Factor extraction. The process of factor extraction involves identifying hypothetical latent variables (factors) that can account mathematically for the patterns of covariation among items. Using the preceding figure as an example, the factor analytic program, in essence, would try to define a mathematical entity (i.e., factor) that would account for the shaded portions of the figure.

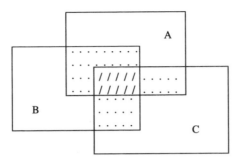

Figure 6.1. Covariation Among Three Hypothetical Items

It might first identify the cross-hashed area, which is common to all three and thus presumably caused by a common latent variable or factor. The cross-hashed area would likely "get the attention" of the factor analytic program because all three items can be explained, at least to some degree, by a factor corresponding to it. For none of the three items is this area irrelevant. In this sense, a factor related to the cross-hashed area may empirically do the best job of explaining variance among the entire set of items. A factor corresponding to the cross-hashed area would, in essence, be a hypothesized latent variable presumed to cause the covariation among the three items depicted by the cross-hashing in the figure. Its relationship to the items would be the same as that of any latent variable to the items it influences. Its path diagram would look like any path diagram for one latent variable and three items:

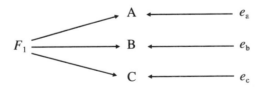

The paths from F_1 to the items would have values (standardized path coefficients) whose products were equal to the correlations between the items. Thus the product of the paths from F_1 to A and from F_1 to B would equal the correlation between A and B.

If the cross-hashed area were removed from the diagram of the over-lapping boxes, there would still be shared variance among the items (i.e., the dotted areas). The factor analytic program could attempt to define another factor based on the *remaining* overlap, or covariation, among the variables. In this case, the shaded area representing the overlap between A and B seems to account for a substantial amount of the remaining shaded area. Therefore, the second factor might be defined as the mathematical entity that explains the covariation corresponding to this area. Note that this shaded area, minus the cross-hashed portion removed by factor 1, does not overlap with C. This means that the second factor would not do a good job of explaining covariation involving item C, but would explain some of the covariation between items A and B.

A path diagram for this two-factor solution would look as follows:

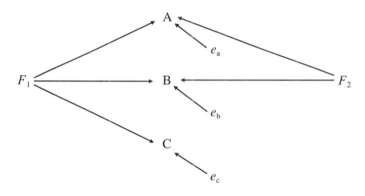

This diagram indicates that Factor 1 (F_1) is a cause of variation in all three items, A, B, and C. Factor 2 (F_2) is a cause of variation in A and B but *not* C. Each of the items has, in addition to the factors, a source of error, or unique, variance that corresponds to the unshaded portions of the "boxes" diagram used to illustrate this example. If this were an actual factor analytic solution, the program would assign values to the paths from the factors to the items. These would be called *factor loadings* and would represent the correlation between each original item and the factor from which the path emanated. Each factor loading would be a standard-ized coefficient for a path running from a factor to an item. As before, the products of the values along the paths connecting items would equal the correlation between those items. However, for each correlation there are now two routes to consider, one involving each factor. For example, the correlation between A and B would equal the product of the paths from F_1 to A and B, respectively, *plus* the product of the paths from F_2 to A and B, respectively.

In actuality, it is unlikely for the value from Factor 2 to item C to be precisely zero. Thus one could argue that a path from Factor 2 to item C should be included in the above figure, even though its numerical value might be very close to zero.

Note that the factors have no meaning at this point. This is generally the case at this stage of any factor analysis. The factors are merely mathematical conveniences invoked to explain covariation among the items. Mathematically and conceptually different factors with different relationships to the items could have been invoked just as readily.

Criteria for extraction. Whether factors beyond the first one are extracted depends on what the factor analyst is seeking. Factor analysis aids the scale developer by quantifying how much of the total variation in the entire set of items can be accounted for as successive factors are added. Ideally, we would like to extract all the *primary factors*—that is, factors that account for important covariation among items. Typically, some portion of the covariation among items will not truly represent latent variables of interest. It will be due to chance or to relatively minor sources of nonrandom covariation that we would just as soon ignore. For example, inconsequential but detectable covariation, presumably due to fatigue, might exist among items occurring near the end of a questionnaire. We might prefer to write off these *secondary factors* as error because they may be uninterpretable or of minor importance.

In practice, the distinction between primary and secondary factors may not be as clear as we would like it to be. For one thing, "irrelevant" sources of variation may be more relevant than we think if they account for a large amount of covariation among items. For example, if fatigue were a major influence in determining how items were answered, we would probably want to know about, and quite possibly quantify, that problem. On the other hand, we might not even be able to name the source of a distinctly minor factor and its explanatory utility might be nil. Retaining it would be nonparsimonious while increasing our understanding little, if at all.

How, then, do we determine which factors deserve our attention and which can be ignored? Different approaches exist for resolving the issue of how many factors to extract from a set of data. Most often, they are based on how good a job a given number of factors does of explaining the total amount of variance (i.e., the collective variance of all the items).

Because of the way factor analysis works, successive factors explain progressively less of the variance than did their immediate predecessors. The analytic method assures that the first factor identified by the analysis is the most important (i.e., explains the most covariation), the second identified is the next most important, and so forth. The trick is to determine the point of diminishing returns. The trade-off is between having a simpler factor structure that allows you to account for the covariance in the original items with as few factors as possible, versus doing a good job of explaining a substantial portion of the total variance in the set of original items. The latter implies more factors whereas the former implies fewer.

Several guidelines have been developed to assist in deciding how many factors to extract. Space does not allow a discussion of each method. Readers should consult the standard factor analytic texts cited earlier for greater detail concerning the appropriate use of these guidelines. However, two widely used criteria are briefly discussed in the following paragraphs.

Kaiser's *eigenvalue rule* (e.g., Nunnally, 1978) is based essentially on retaining only factors that explain more variance than the average amount explained by one of the original items. (Strictly speaking, this interpretation of the eigenvalue rule applies only to one type of factors called "principal components." However, it is applicable in spirit to other types of factors as well.) The logic behind Kaiser's method is as follows: If the worst factor explains more variance than an original item, then one is achieving some degree of condensation (i.e., the ability to explain variation with a set of factors smaller than the original number of items). If one or more factors are actually explaining less variance than an item, then nothing is gained by retaining them.

Cattell's (1966) *scree test* is another widely used factor extraction criterion. The name is based on an analogy between the debris, called scree, that collects at the bottom of a hill after a landslide, and the relatively meaningless factors that result from overextraction. Cattell recommends plotting the amount of variance explained by each successive factor. A scree plot consists of a vertical axis corresponding to eigenvalues, a horizontal axis corresponding to successive factors, and numerical markers, plotted on these axes, indicating the eigenvalues corresponding to each factor. Because each factor explains less variance than the preceding factors, an imaginary line connecting the markers for successive factors generally runs from the top left of the graph to the bottom right (see Figure 6.2).

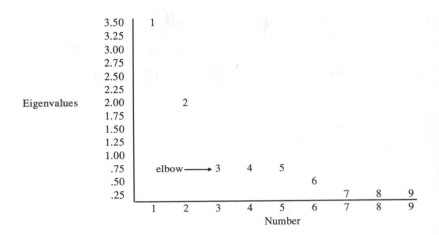

Figure 6.2. Scree Plot Showing Distinct Elbow

If there is a point below which factors explain relatively little variance and above which they explain substantially more, this usually appears as an "elbow" in the plot (the point labeled "3" in Figure 6.2). This plot bears some physical resemblance to the profile of a hillside. The portion beyond the elbow (factors 3 through 9 in Figure 6.2) corresponds to the rubble, or scree, that gathers. Cattell's guidelines call for retaining factors above the elbow (the first two, in this case) and rejecting those below it. This amounts to keeping the factors that contribute most to the explanation of variance in the total set of original items. Unfortunately, some scree plots do not have as obvious an elbow as one would like (as in Figure 6.3). Therefore, this criterion for selecting how many factors to retain is somewhat subjective.

Both Kaiser's and Cattell's criteria are based on the magnitude of factors' eigenvalues, which are a means of expressing how much variance the factors explain. Zwick and Velicer (1986) examined the effect of different criteria for extracting factors. To do this, they "manufactured" a data set based on an actual predetermined factor structure. They knew exactly what the true scores of the underlying latent variables were, because they had built the data set to their specifications rather than collecting data from subjects. Some rather specialized techniques not available on most computer packages did the best job of indicating how many factors to extract. The eigenvalue rule generally resulted in extracting too many factors, confirming a suspicion shared by

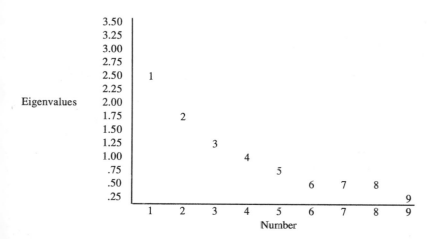

Figure 6.3. Scree Plot Without a Distinct Elbow

many investigators. Of the methods that are readily available and easy to perform, the inspection of a scree plot fared reasonably well. Although this method is far from perfect, and clearly not as good as some less readily available alternatives, it provides an acceptable starting point for determining how many factors to extract from a data set.

Criteria for determining how many latent variables underlie a data set, and thus how many factors to extract, clearly are useful aids. However, much of this process is art, and experience is an invaluable guide. The meaning or interpretability of the resultant factors provides important clues about how many to retain.

Factor rotation. At the point where a number of factors has been extracted from the covariance matrix in accordance with some criterion for retention, two of the three purposes listed earlier for factor analysis have been achieved. For instance, in the case of our 3-item hypothetical example, we have decided how many latent variables to extract (two) and, in so doing, have achieved condensation (though not much, in this case) relative to the original set of items. I have stated earlier that these factors are merely arbitrary, hypothetical, mathematical conveniences. If the factors are arbitrary, how can we learn about the nature of the latent variables underlying the set of items? To accomplish this third purpose, factor analysts typically perform a factor rotation. This process involves considering alternative sets of factors that do an equally good job, mathematically, of defining covariation among the original items but that differ in the conceptual insights they offer the investigator.

A goal of factor rotation is to find a set of arbitrary factors that provides the clearest conceptual picture of the relationships among the items by approximating *simple structure*. Simple structure is attained if each of the original items relates to (i.e., loads on) one, and only one, factor. This would be the case if each item had factor loadings of zero on all but one factor. Then a subset of the original items would be exclusively associated with Factor 1, another subset would be exclusively associated with Factor 2, and so on, depending on how many factors had been extracted. This is useful conceptually because it makes it much easier to determine what the latent variable is that each factor represents.

A spatial analogy to factor analysis and rotation. To clarify how rotation can imbue arbitrary factors with meaning, let us consider a simple spatial example involving a circular piece of paper on which a floor plan of a building has been drawn. Let us assume that the floor plan is of a school that consists of a long corridor with classrooms on either side. Because the drawing is two-dimensional, we could draw two axes at right angles to one another on the floor plan and define coordinates in reference to these axes. How these axes are oriented relative to the floor plan is irrelevant. Any location on the plan (e.g., the location of any room in the building) can be specified in terms of units on each of the two axes. Beyond providing a frame of reference for describing the spatial relationships among the various rooms, the axes have no inherent meaning. However, it may be useful to re-orient the axes in some specific way. For example, having one axis (call it the longitudinal axis) run parallel to the long corridor of the building would result in a correspondence between values along that axis and room numbers. This imbues the previously meaningless axis with some informational content that corresponds to how the building is laid out. The perpendicular (lateral) axis would then run across the building, from the windows on one side of the building, through the corridor, and over to the windows on the other side. This is also "meaningful" in that proximity to a window or to the corridor is often used by teachers and students to identify locations within a room. The values on the lateral axis would locate a point as being near the left-side windows, near the corridor, or near the right-side windows. Alternatively, a north-south and east-west orientation for the axes might be useful. Once again, this would give meaning to what had been heretofore meaningless reference axes. Unless the long corridor happened to fall along one of the major map directions, these two alternative orientations for reference axes would differ. In each case, the axes would have meaning in terms of some external phenomenon (either building layout or compass directions), but the meanings would be different. Which would be preferable would depend on what uses were intended for the floor plan. If the plan were to be used for planning fire drills, the corridor orientation would seem best. For example, the exit paths could be described as entailing moving along the lateral axis to the main corridor and then moving along the longitudinal axis to an exit. If the floorplan were to be utilized for determining the extent of passive solar heating, the map-directions orientation would be preferable. For example, windows facing south could be unshaded in cool weather and shaded in warm. In both examples, rotating a set of arbitrary reference axes imbued them with "real world" meaning without altering their usefulness as a basis for a coordinate system to describe any point on the floor plan.

This relationship of meaningful spatial referents to the axes is analogous to the relationships of items to factors when simple structure is attained. With simple structure, one set of similar items (analogous to rooms) is highly correlated with values of a single dimension (the longitudinal axis) and is uncorrelated to values of other dimensions (the lateral axis). A second homogenous grouping of items (analogous to location near a window versus near the corridor) is independent of values for the first factor (analogous to the longitudinal axis) but strongly related to values of the second (lateral axis).

Another point worth noting from our spatial example is that the axes drawn on the floor plan were perpendicular to one another. This means that location on one axis could not be inferred from location on the other. Stated differently, information about values on one axis was independent of information about values on the other. There was no redundancy between the two axes. If you knew the location of an object with respect to one of the axes, learning its value relative to the other axis would be all new information. Knowing how far down the corridor a particular student's desk was located told you nothing about its proximity to the window. Keeping factors perpendicular (i.e., statistically independent) with respect to one another in the process of rotation results in *orthogonal* factors. When this is done, the true value of an item on any given factor is independent of its true value on any other factor that has been extracted. Knowing an item's value on one tells you nothing about its value on any other factor. This independence of factors is preserved when they are rotated, unless the analyst chooses explicitly to do otherwise.

Alternatively, factors can be rotated so that the axis corresponding to each successive factor is fitted optimally without the constraint of keeping them perpendicular. This is called an *oblique* rotation. Orthogonal factors, because of their statistical independence, possess a simplicity and elegance that oblique factors do not. For example, information about the location of a point with respect to the lateral factor in the school floor plan example was not at all redundant with information based on the longitudinal axis. In some situations, being able to fit axes precisely to locations of interest might supersede the desire for the simplicity of orthogonal factors. If, for example, there were a reason to specify locations in the school with respect to location along the corridor and location along a north-south axis, these two nonperpendicular references could be used. Any point on the floor plan could still be specified in terms of values along these two axes. However, some redundancy might exist. For example, moving down the corridor or heading south might both bring you closer to the front entrance. Factor analytic texts (e.g., Cureton, 1983; Gorsuch 1983; Harman, 1976; or McDonald, 1984) provide a more comprehensive treatment of how to choose and perform orthogonal versus oblique rotations.

USING FACTOR ANALYSIS IN
SCALE DEVELOPMENT

An example should make inspecting a scree plot and examining the loadings for rotated factors less abstract. Some colleagues and I (DeVellis, DeVellis, Blanchard, Klotz, Luchok, & Voyce, 1990) developed a scale assessing parents' beliefs about who or what influences their children's health. Although the full scale has 30 items and assesses several aspects of these beliefs, for this presentation I will discuss only 12 of the items:

1. I have the ability to influence my child's well-being.
2. Whether my child avoids injury is just a matter of luck.
3. Luck plays a big part in determining how healthy my child is.
4. I can do a lot to prevent my child from getting hurt.
5. I can do a lot to prevent my child from getting sick.
6. Whether my child avoids sickness is just a matter of luck.
7. The things I do at home with my child are an important part of my child' well-being.
8. My child's safety depends on me.
9. I can do a lot to help my child stay well.

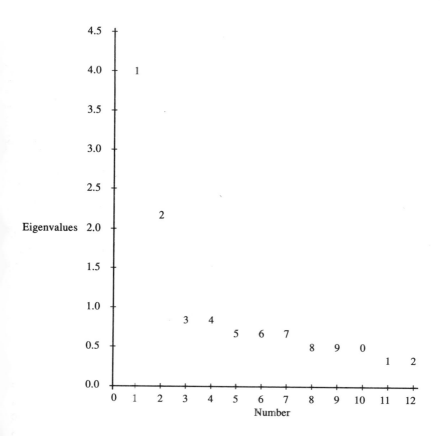

Figure 6.4. Scree Plot From Factor Analysis of Belief Items

10. My child's good health is largely a matter of good fortune.
11. I can do a lot to help my child be strong and healthy.
12. Whether my child stays healthy or gets sick is just a matter of fate.

These items were administered to 396 parents, and the resultant data were factor analyzed. The first objective of the factor analysis was to determine how many factors there were underlying the items. SAS-PC was used to perform the factor analysis and a scree plot was requested. A scree plot similar to the type printed by SAS appears in Figure 6.4. Note that 12 factors (i.e., as many as the number of items) are plotted. However, two of those are located on the initial portion of the plot and

Table 6.1

Rotated Factor Pattern

	Factor 1	Factor 2
ITEM 9	0.78612	–0.22093
ITEM 11	0.74807	–0.18546
ITEM 4	0.71880	–0.02282
ITEM 5	0.65897	–0.15802
ITEM 7	0.65814	0.01909
ITEM 1	0.59749	–0.14053
ITEM 8	0.51857	–0.07419
ITEM 6	–0.09218	0.82181
ITEM 10	–0.10873	0.78587
ITEM 3	–0.07773	0.75370
ITEM 12	–0.17298	0.73783
ITEM 2	–0.11609	0.63583

the remainder form the scree running along its bottom. This strongly suggests that two factors account for much of the variation among the items.

Having determined how many factors to retain, we reran the program specifying 2 factors and *varimax* rotation. Varimax, so named because it *max*imizes the *vari*ance of squared loadings (i.e., correlations of items with factors), is the most common orthogonal rotation method. (The factor analysis texts cited earlier discuss alternative rotation methods using other optimization criteria.) Had we failed to approximate simple structure, we might have performed an oblique rotation to improve the fit between items and factors. However, in this case, the simpler orthogonal rotation yielded meaningful item groupings and strong, unambiguous loadings.

This is evident from the table of factor loadings in Table 6.1. Each row contains the loadings of a given item on the two factors. An option available in SAS has reordered the items in the table so that those with high loadings on each factor are grouped together.

In this table, factor loadings greater than 0.50 have been italicized. Each factor is defined by the items that load most heavily on it (i.e., those italicized). By referring to the content of those items, one can discern the nature of the latent variable that each factor represents. In this case, all of the items loading strongly on Factor 1 concern the parent as an influence over whether a child remains safe and healthy. Those loading

Table 6.2

Cronbach Coefficient Alpha

for RAW variables: 0.796472			for STANDARDIZED variables: .802006	
	Raw Variables		Standardized Variables	
Deleted Variable	Correlation with Total	Alpha	Correlation with Total	Alpha
Item 9	0.675583	0.741489	0.676138	0.749666
Item 11	0.646645	0.748916	0.644648	0.755695
Item 5	0.545751	0.770329	0.535924	0.775939
Item 4	0.562833	0.763252	0.572530	0.769222
Item 7	0.466433	0.782509	0.474390	0.787007
Item 8	0.409650	0.793925	0.404512	0.799245
Item 1	0.437088	0.785718	0.440404	0.793003

primarily on Factor 2, on the other hand, concern the influence of luck or fate on the child's health.

These two homogenous item sets can be examined further. For example, alpha could be computed for each grouping. Computing alpha on these item groupings using SAS-PC yields the results in Tables 6.2 and 6.3.

Both scales have acceptable alpha reliability coefficients. Note that the SAS-PC CORR procedure calculates alpha for unstandardized and standardized items. The latter calculation is equivalent to using the correlation-based alpha formula. For both scales, these two methods of computing alpha yield quite similar values. Note also that for neither scale would alpha increase by dropping any item. Alphas nearly as high as those obtained for the full scales result from dropping one item (i.e., item 8 from scale 1 and item 2 from scale 2). However, retaining these items provides a bit of additional insurance that the reliability will not drop below acceptable levels on a new sample and does not increase the scales' length significantly.

All of the caveats applicable to scales in general at this point in their development are applicable to factor analytically derived scales. For example, it is very important to replicate the scales' reliability using an independent sample. In fact, it probably would be useful to replicate the whole factor analytic process on an independent sample to demonstrate that the results obtained were not a one-time chance occurrence.

Table 6.3

Cronbach Coefficient Alpha

for RAW variables: 0.811162			for STANDARDIZED variables: 0.811781	
	Raw Variables		Standardized Variables	
Deleted	*Correlation*		*Correlation*	
Variable	*with Total*	*Alpha*	*with Total*	*Alpha*
Item 6	0.684085	0.748385	0.682663	0.749534
Item 3	0.596210	0.775578	0.594180	0.776819
Item 10	0.636829	0.762590	0.639360	0.763036
Item 12	0.593667	0.776669	0.592234	0.777405
Item 2	0.491460	0.806544	0.493448	0.806449

Sample size. The likelihood of a factor structure replicating is at least partially a function of the sample size used in the original analysis. In general, the factor pattern that emerges from a large-sample factor analysis will be more stable than that emerging from a smaller sample. Inevitably, the question arises, "How large is large enough?" This is a question that is difficult to answer. As with many other statistical procedures, both the relative (i.e., to the number of variables analyzed) and the absolute number of subjects should be considered. The larger the number of items to be factored and the larger the number of factors anticipated, the more subjects should be included in the analysis. It is tempting, based on this fact, to seek a standard ratio of subjects to items. However, as the sample gets progressively larger, the ratio of subjects to items can safely diminish. For a 20-item factor analysis, 100 subjects would probably be too few, but for a 90-item factor analysis, 400 might be adequate. Tinsley and Tinsley (1987) suggest a ratio of about 5 to 10 subjects per item, up to about 300 subjects. They suggest that when the sample is as large as 300, the ratio can be relaxed. In the same article they cite another set of guidelines, attributed to Comrey (1973), that classifies a sample of 100 as poor, 200 as fair, 300 as good, 500 as very good, and 1,000 as excellent. More recently, Comrey (1988) stated that a sample size of 200 is adequate in most cases of ordinary factor analysis that involve no more than 40 items. It is certainly not uncommon to see factor analyses used in scale development based on more modest samples (e.g., 150 subjects). However, the point is well taken that larger samples increase the generalizability of the conclusions reached by means of factor analysis. Of course, replicating a factor analytic solution on a separate sample may be the best means of demonstrating its generalizability.

Factor analysis and validity. Factor analytic methods can also be used in scale validation. For example, items from new scales could be factor analyzed along with items of established scales measuring either the same or different constructs. If items from the new scales load on different factors than items from established scales of different constructs, this would provide evidence of *discriminant validity*. Conversely, if the items from a new scale loaded on the same factor as the items of an established measure of the same construct, this would be evidence of *convergent validity*. Even if no established scales are factored along with the new scale items, factor analysis can provide validity information. For example, if anticipated item groupings are identified prior to factoring, a factor analytic solution that is consistent with these groupings is evidence of *factorial validity* (Comrey, 1988).

It is important to recognize that factor analysis tells us about the latent variables underlying our *set of items,* not necessarily the concept we assume them to operationalize. Thus returning to an earlier example, a factor analysis that yields three factors underlying 25 affect items is not addressing the nature of affect per se. It is merely telling us what the empirical relationships are among a specific set of items; that is, it speaks to the *operationalization* of the construct but not necessarily to the construct itself.

CONFIRMATORY FACTOR ANALYSIS

For the most part, the factor analytic methods we have discussed have left the task of defining the factors up to the factor analysis program. However, in the context of scale development, we have a fairly clear idea at the outset about what factors we think underlie the items. Presumably, the items were originally written or selected with the intention of capturing specific latent variables. If we developed a pool of items carefully using the methods described earlier, why would we need factor analysis to tell us what the items have in common? There are at least two answers to this question. First, we may want confirmation that the number of latent variables underlying the items corresponds to the number we expect. Second, as discussion of factorial validity suggested, if the factor analysis "discovers" precisely the item groupings that we intended when creating the items, we have strong confirmation of our initial hypothesis concerning how the items should relate to one another. In essence, the factor analysis would have been used to confirm an expected factor structure rather than to determine a structure that was previously unknown.

There is another factor analytic strategy that is even more explicitly confirmatory. This technique involves specifying a priori which items should group together as indicators of shared latent variables. In this type of analysis, the investigator explicates the desired factor structure when submitting the data for factor analysis and the program provides an indication of how well the actual data conform to the specified factor pattern. The methods used in this type of confirmatory factor analysis differ from conventional factor analytic methods and usually require specialized computer programs. Long (1983) discusses confirmatory analyses in detail. Confirmatory procedures can certainly be useful. Note, however, that a scale developer can have in mind which items should group together without explicitly programming this information into the analysis (i.e., without using formally confirmatory methods). Factor analytically derived groupings can still be compared to these a priori item groupings, and this requires only the conventional (i.e., nonconfirmatory) factor analytic methods that we have discussed throughout this chapter. Furthermore, finding by means of conventional factoring methods that items group together as suspected should be even more reassuring to the investigator because the analysis has not been instructed to "look for" a specific pattern. Instead, it has found the anticipated pattern on its own.

CONCLUSIONS

Factor analytic methods are an important adjunct to other scale development procedures. They are particularly useful in determining how many factors, and hence how many latent variables, underlie a set of items. They also can help the investigator determine whether latent variables other than the ones expected seem to explain the variation in the items. Factor analysis also can help to identify potentially problematic items, although other methods discussed in Chapter 5, such as item-scale correlations and the effects of item inclusion/exclusion on coefficient alpha, also should be used.

The examination of factor analysis in this book has been far from comprehensive. Of necessity, many issues that are important but inappropriate for inclusion here have not been covered. Readers who wish to take the next step in learning about factor analysis are referred to several sources, including those cited earlier in this chapter. Nunnally (1978) provides a very useful introduction to factor analysis, including a description of how to extract factors by the "centroid method" using only a hand calculator. This exercise, although somewhat anachronistic in light of the myriad computer packages available, is an excellent way to develop a working familiarity with factor analytic methods. Tinsley and Tinsley (1987) have written a brief but highly informative article that provides an overview of factor analytic concepts. Two brief volumes by Kim and Mueller (1978a, 1978b) provide a concise yet fairly detailed introduction to this topic. Comrey (1988) has written an article, suitable for readers with a limited background in factor analysis, specifically discussing its uses in scale development. Each of these sources, in turn, includes numerous references to more advanced texts and papers.

EXERCISES

1. If an investigator suspects that a fairly large set of items has more than one underlying latent variable, why would computing alpha on the whole set of items be problematic?

2. In what sense does factor analysis condense information?

3. What is a correlation between an item and a factor called?

4. For a series of successively extracted factors, what is the relationship between factors in the amount of variance in the original item set that each factor explains?

5. How do primary and secondary factors differ?

6. How is a scree plot used to determine how many factors to retain?

7. Give an example of a factor pattern table, for 10 items loading on two factors, that illustrates simple structure.

8. What is the primary difference between orthogonal and oblique factor rotation methods?

9. Explain the meaning of factorial validity.

7

Measurement in the Broader Research Context

The opening chapter of this volume set the stage for what was to follow by providing some examples of when and why measurement issues arise, discussing the role of theory in measurement, and emphasizing the false economy of skimping on measurement procedures. In essence, it sketched the larger context of research before the focus shifted to the specific issues covered in later chapters. This chapter returns to the big picture and looks briefly at the scale within the larger context of an investigation.

In reexamining the broader context of research, I highlight selected issues. Measurement intersects with a wide array of research issues. Discussing all these points of intersection, even superficially, would easily fill a volume. Instead, I will provide some examples of the types of issues a researcher should keep in mind when shifting attention from the development of a scale per se to its use in a substantive research context.

To make the discussion a bit more concrete, let us return to the example from the first chapter of the marketing team that believed that parental aspirations exerted a strong influence over the decision to purchase toys appearing to be educationally valuable. Assume that the researchers have developed a scale and are reasonably confident that it accurately measures parental aspirations. Assume further that they have a clear understanding of how these aspirations relate to purchasing decisions. How do they go about using the scale?

BEFORE THE SCALE ADMINISTRATION

The researchers must decide on the *mode of scale administration*. For example, they might consider using it as part of an interview rather than a printed questionnaire. It is important to recognize that a scale intended to be completed in print form may have substantially different properties when the items and responses are presented orally. For example, parents might be more reluctant to acknowledge high aspirations if they had to report them aloud to an interviewer rather than marking a response option.

(Investigators contemplating the use of orally administered questionnaires should consult Dillman, 1978, and the volumes in the Applied Social Research Methods series by Lavrakas, 1987, and Fowler & Mangione, 1989.) Generally, it is wise to restrict the mode of administering a new scale to the method used during scale development. A G-study may be used to determine the scale's generalizability across administration modes (see Chapter 6).

Another important issue is the *context of the scale*. What questions will precede the scale itself? How will these questions affect responses to the scale? Nunnally (1978, pp. 627-677) refers to contextual factors such as response styles, fatigue, and motivation as *contingent variables*. He also points out that they can adversely affect research in three ways: (a) by reducing the reliability of scales; (b) by constituting reliable sources of variation other than the construct of interest, thus lowering validity; and (c) by altering the relationships among variables, making them appear, for example, to be more highly correlated than they actually are. As an example of how contingent variables might operate, consider *mood induction* and *cognitive sets* as they might apply to the marketing research example. The former might be an issue if, for example, the market researchers decided to include a depression or self-esteem scale in the same questionnaire as their aspirations scale. Scales tapping these (and other) constructs often contain items that express negative views of one's self. The Rosenberg Self-Esteem scale (Rosenberg, 1965), for example, contains such items as, "I feel I do not have much to be proud of" (as well as items expressing a positive self-appraisal). A researcher who was not sensitive to the potential effects of mood induction might select a series of exclusively self-critical items to accompany a newly developed scale. Reading statements that consistently express negative assessments of one's self may induce a dysphoric state that, in turn, can cause whatever follows to be perceived differently than it would otherwise (e.g., Rholes, Riskind, & Lane, 1987). This might have each of the three adverse effects noted by Nunnally. Accordingly, in the presence of affectively negative items, aspiration items might take on a somewhat different shade of meaning, thus lowering the proportion of variance in those items that is attributable to the intended latent variable. Or, in an extreme instance, some items from the aspiration scale might come to be influenced primarily by the induced mood state, rendering the scale multifactorial and lowering its validity as a measure of parental aspiration. Finally, to the extent that respondents' mood affected their responses to the aspiration items, scores for this scale might correlate artificially highly with other mood-related measures.

Cognitive sets are a more general example of the same phenomenon; that is, some frame of reference other than mood might be induced by focusing respondents' attention on a specific topic. For example, immediately preceding the scale with items concerning the respondents' income, the value of their home, and the amount they spend annually on various categories of consumer goods might create a mental set that temporarily altered their aspirations for their children. As a result, the responses to the scale might reflect an untended transient state. As with mood, this cognitive set might adversely affect the reliability and/or validity of the scale by contaminating the extent to which it unambiguously reflects parental aspirations.

AFTER THE SCALE ADMINISTRATION

A quite different set of issues emerges after the scale has been used to address a substantive research question. The primary concerns at this point are analysis and interpretation of data generated by the instrument.

Analytic issues. One issue in data analysis is the appropriateness of various techniques for variables with different scaling properties. The theoretical perspective and methods advocated most strongly in this book should result in scales that are amenable to a wide variety of data analytic methods. Although, strictly speaking, items using Likert or semantic differential response formats may be ordinal, a wealth of accumulated experience supports applying interval-based analytic methods to the scales they yield. Nunnally (1978) "strongly believes that it is permissible to treat most of the measurement methods in psychology and other behavioral sciences as leading to interval scales," and argues that "no harm is done in most studies in the behavioral sciences by employing methods of mathematical and statistical analysis which take intervals seriously" (p. 17). However, the question of what methods are best suited to what types of data has been, and certainly will continue to be, hotly debated in the social sciences. Perhaps the most practical approach is to monitor (and conform to) the prevailing sentiment with respect to this issue in one's area of interest. For now, a perspective similar to that of Nunnally seems to influence the majority of behavioral researchers.

Interpretation issues. Assuming that the researcher has arrived at a suitable analytic plan for the data generated by a newly developed scale, the question of how to interpret the data remains. One point to keep in mind at this juncture is that the validity of a scale is not firmly established during scale development. Validation is a cumulative, ongoing process. Especially if the results appear strongly counterintuitive or countertheoretical, the researcher must consider the possibility that the scale is invalid in the context of that particular study (if not more broadly). It may be that the extent to which the validity of the scale generalizes across populations, settings, specific details of administration, or an assortment of other dimensions is limited. For example, the hypothetical parental aspiration measure might have been developed with a relatively affluent population in mind and its validity for individuals whose resources are more limited may be unacceptable. Any conclusions based on a scale that has had limited use should consider the following: (a) how its present application differs from the context of its original validation, (b) the likelihood that these differences might limit the validity of the scale, and (c) the implications of these limitations for the present research.

FINAL THOUGHTS

Measurement is a vital aspect of social and behavioral research. The careful design, assessment, and application of measurement scales enables researchers to focus on the (often unobservable) variables of primary interest and to develop the clearest understanding of the relationships among these variables. Poor measurement, on the other hand, shrouds research in a veil of ambiguity. The uncertainty that it creates can undermine an otherwise impeccably designed and executed study. Viewed in this light, the efforts entailed in careful measurement are amply rewarded by their benefits.

References

Ajzen, I., & Fishbein, M. (1980). *Understanding attitudes and predicting behavior.* Englewood Cliffs, NJ: Prentice-Hall.

Allen, M. J., & Yen, W. M. (1979). *Introduction to measurement theory.* Monterey: Brooks/Cole.

Anastasi, A. (1968). *Psychological testing* (3rd ed.).New York: Macmillan.

Asher, H. B. (1983). *Causal modeling* (2nd ed.). Sage University Paper Series on Quantitative Application in the Social Sciences, Series No. 07-003. Beverly Hills, CA: Sage.

Barnette, W. L. (1976). *Readings in psychological tests and measurements* (3rd. ed.). Baltimore: Williams & Wilkins.

Blalock, S. J., DeVellis, R. F., Brown, G. K., & Wallston, K. A. (1989). Validity of the Center for Epidemiological Studies Depression scale in arthritis populations. *Arthritis and Rheumatism, 32,* 991-997.

Bohrnstedt, G. W. (1969). A quick method for determining the reliability and validity of multiple-item scales. *American Sociological Review, 34,* 542-548.

Bollen, K. A. (1989). *Structural equations with latent variables.* New York: John Wiley.

Campbell, D. T., & Fiske, D. W. (1959). Convergent and discriminant validation by the multitrait-multimethod matrix. *Psychological Bulletin, 56,* 81-105.

Carmines, E. G., & McIver, J. P. (1981). Analyzing models with unobserved variables: Analysis of covariance structures. In G. W. Bohrnstedt and E. F. Borgatta (Eds.), *Social measurement: Current issues* (pp. 65-115). Beverly Hills, CA: Sage.

Cattell, R. B. (1966). The scree test for the number of factors. *Multivariate Behavioral Research, 1,* 245-276.

Comrey, A. L. (1973). *A first course in factor analysis.* New York: Academic Press.

Comrey, A. L. (1988). Factor analytic methods of scale development in personality and clinical psychology. *Journal of Consulting and Clinical Psychology, 56,* 754-761.

Converse, J. M., & Presser, S. (1986). *Survey Questions: Handcrafting the standardized questionnaire.* Sage University Paper Series on Quantitative Application in the Social Sciences, Series No. 07-063. Beverly Hills, CA: Sage.

Crocker, L., & Algina, J. (1986). *Introduction to classical and modern test theory.* New York: Holt, Rinehart & Winston.

Cronbach, L. J. (1951). Coefficient alpha and the internal structure of tests. *Psychometrika, 16,* 297-334.

Cronbach, L. J., Gleser, G. C., Nanda, H., & Rajaratnam, N. (1972). *Dependability of behavioral measurements: Theory of generalizability for scores and profiles.* New York: John Wiley.

Cronbach, L. J., & Meehl, P. E. (1955). Construct validity in psychological tests. *Psychological Bulletin, 52,* 281-302.

Cureton, E. E. (1983). *Factor analysis: An applied approach.* Hillsdale, NJ: Lawrence Erlbaum.

Dale, F., & Chall, J. E. (1948). A formula for predicting readability: Instructions. *Education Research Bulletin, 27,* 37-54.

DeVellis, R. F., DeVellis, B. M., Blanchard, L. W., Klotz, M. L., Luchok, K., & Voyce, C. (1990). *Development and validation of the Parent Health Locus of Control (PHLOC) scales.* Unpublished manuscript, University of North Carolina at Chapel Hill.

DeVellis, R. F., DeVellis, B. M., Revicki, D. A., Lurie, S. J., Runyan, D. K., & Bristol, M. M. (1985). Development and validation of the child improvement locus of control (CILC) scales. *Journal of Social and Clinical Psychology, 3,* 307-324.

DeVellis, R. F., Holt, K., Renner, B. R., Blalock, S. J., Blanchard, L. W., Cook, H. L., Klotz, M. L., Mikow, V., & Harring, K. (1990). The relationship of social comparison to rheumatoid arthritis symptoms and affect. *Basic and Applied Social Psychology, 11,* 1-18.

Dillman, D. A. (1978). *Mail and telephone surveys: The total design method.* New York: Wiley-Interscience.

Duncan, O. D. (1975). *Introduction to structural equation models.* New York: Academic Press.

Duncan, O. D. (1984). *Notes on social measurement: Historical and critical* New York: Russell Sage.

Festinger, L. (1954). A theory of social comparison processes. *Human Relations, 7,* 117-140.

Fowler, F. J. (1988). *Survey research methods.* Beverly Hills, CA: Sage.

Fowler, F. J., & Mangione, T. W. (1989). *Standardized survey interviewing.* Beverly Hills, CA: Sage.

Fry, E. (1977). Fry's readability graph: Clarifications, validity, and extension to level 17. *Journal of Reading, 21,* 249.

Gerrity, M. S., DeVellis, R. F., & Earp, J. A. (1990). Physicians' reactions to uncertainty in patient care: A new measure and new insights. *Medical Care, 28,* 724-736.

Ghiselli, E. E., Campbell, J. P., & Zedeck, S. (1981). *Measurement theory for the behavioral sciences.* San Francisco: Freeman.

Gorsuch, R. L. (1983). *Factor analysis.* Hillsdale, NJ: Lawrence Erlbaum.

Harman, H. H. (1976). *Modern factor analysis.* Chicago: University of Chicago Press.

Hathaway, S. R., & McKinley, J. C. (1967). *Minnesota Multiphasic Personality Inventory: Manual for administration and scoring.* New York: Psychological Corporation.

Hathaway, S. R., & Meehl, P. E. (1951). *An atlas for the clinical use of the MMPI.* Minneapolis: University of Minnesota Press.

Jöreskog, K. G. (1971). Simultaneous factor analysis in several populations. *Psychometrika, 36,* 109-134.

Kelly, J. R., & McGrath, J. E. (1988). *On time and method.* Beverly Hills, CA: Sage.

Kenny, D. A. (1979). "Correlation and causality. New York: John Wiley.

Kim, J., & Mueller, C. W. (1978a). *Introduction to factor analysis: What it is and how to do it.* Sage University Paper Series on Quantitative Applications in the Social Sciences, Series No. 07-013. Beverly Hills, CA: Sage.

Kim, J., & Mueller, C. W. (1978b). *Factor analysis: Statistical methods and practical issues.* Sage University Paper Series on Quantitative Applications in the Social Sciences, Series No. 07-014. Beverly Hills, CA: Sage.

Lavrakas, P. J. (1987). *Telephone survey methods.* Beverly Hills, CA: Sage.

Levenson, H. (1973). Multidimensional locus of control in psychiatric patients. *Journal of Consulting and Clinical Psychology, 41,* 397-404.

Lipsey, M. W. (1990). *Design sensitivity: Statistical power for experimental research.* Beverly Hills, CA: Sage.

Long, J. S. (1983). *Confirmatory factor analysis.* Sage University Paper Series on Quantitative Applications in the Social Sciences, Series No. 07-033. Beverly Hills, CA: Sage.

Lord, F. M., & Novick, M. R. (1968). *Statistical theories of mental test scores.* Reading, MA: Addison-Wesley.

Mayer, J. M. (1978). Assessment of depression. In M. P. McReynolds (Ed.), *Advances in psychological assessment* (Vol. 4, pp. 358-425). San Francisco: Jossey-Bass.

McDonald, R. P. (1984). *Factor analysis and related methods.* Hillsdale, NJ: Lawrence Erlbaum.

Mitchell, S. K. (1979). Interobserver agreement, reliability, and generalizability of data collected in observational studies. *Psychological Bulletin, 86,* 376-390.

Myers, J. L. (1979). *Fundamentals of experimental design* (3rd ed.). Boston: Allyn & Bacon.

Namboodiri, K. (1984). *Matrix algebra: An introduction.* Sage University Paper Series on Quantitative Applications in the Social Sciences, Series No. 07-028. Beverly Hills, CA: Sage.

Narens, L., & Luce, R. D. (1986). Measurement: The theory of numerical assignments. *Psychological Bulletin, 99,* 166-180.

Nunnally, J. C. (1978). *Psychometric theory* (2nd ed.). New York: McGraw-Hill.

Osgood, C. E., & Tannenbaum, P. H. (1955). The principle of congruence in the prediction of attitude change. *Psychological Bulletin, 62,* 42-55.

Radloff, L. (1977). The CES-D scale: A self-report depression scale for research in the general population. *Applied Psychological Measurement, 1,* 385-401.

Reiser, M. (1981). Latent trait modeling of attitude items. In G. W. Bohrnstedt and E. F. Borgatta (Eds.), *Social measurement: Current issues* (pp. 117-144). Beverly Hills, CA: Sage.

Rholes, W. S., Riskind, J. H., & Lane, J. W. (1987). Emotional states and memory biases: Effects of cognitive priming and mood. *Journal of Personality and Social Psychology, 52,* 91-99.

Rosenberg, M. (1965). *Society and the adolescent self-image.* Princeton, NJ: Princeton University Press.

Rotter, J. B. (1966). Generalized expectancies for internal vs external control of reinforcement. *Psychological Monographs, 80* (1, Whole No. 609).

Spielberger, C. D., Gorsuch, R. L., & Lushene, R. E. (1970). *State-trait anxiety inventory (STAI) test manual for form X.* Palo Alto, CA: Consulting Psychologist Press.

Strahan, R., & Gerbasi, K. (1972). Short, homogenous version of the Marlowe-Crowne Social Desirability Scale. *Journal of Clinical Psychology, 28,* 191-193.

Tinsley, H. E. A., & Tinsley, D. J. (1987). Uses of factor analysis in counseling psychology research. *Journal of Counseling Psychology, 34,* 414-424.

Wallston, B. S., Alagna, S. W., DeVellis, B. M., & DeVellis, R. F. (1983). Social support and physical health. *Health Psychology, 2,* 367-391.

Wallston, K. A., Wallston, B. S., & DeVellis, R. (1978). Development and validation of the multidimensional health locus of control (MHLC) scales. *Health Education Monographs, 6,* 161-170.

Zuckerman, M. (1983). The distinction between trait and state scales is not arbitrary: Comment on Allen and Potkay's "On the arbitrary distinction between traits and states." *Journal of Personality and Social Psychology, 44,* 1083-1086.

Zwick, W. R., & Velicer, W. F. (1986). Comparison of five rules for determining the number of components to retain. *Psychological Bulletin, 99,* 432-442.

Index

About the Author

Robert F. DeVellis received his undergraduate degree in psychology from the University of Massachusetts, his M.A. in clinical psychological research from Connecticut College, and his Ph.D. in social psychology from Peabody College. Since 1978 he has been at the University of North Carolina at Chapel Hill, where he is Assistant Director of the Rehabilitation Program in the School of Medicine, Research Associate Professor of Health Behavior and Health Education in the School of Public Health, and Co-Director of Social and Behavioral Sciences Research for the UNC Thurston Arthritis Center. He also holds an appointment in the Psychology Department and is an Associate of the UNC Health Services Research Center. As a graduate student, he worked with Ken and Barbara Wallston on the development of the Multidimensional Health Locus of Control Scales. Since then, he has played a primary or significant role in the development of seven additional scales.